MASTERY IN PRIMARY SCIENCE

Sara Miller McCune founded SAGE Publishing in 1965 to support the dissemination of usable knowledge and educate a global community. SAGE publishes more than 1000 journals and over 800 new books each year, spanning a wide range of subject areas. Our growing selection of library products includes archives, data, case studies and video. SAGE remains majority owned by our founder and after her lifetime will become owned by a charitable trust that secures the company's continued independence.

Los Angeles | London | New Delhi | Singapore | Washington DC | Melbourne

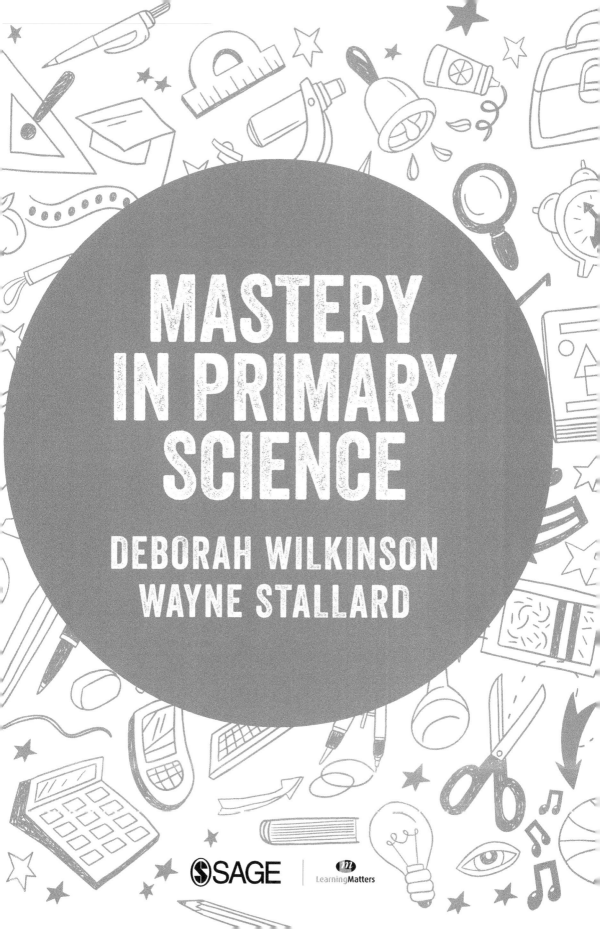

MASTERY IN PRIMARY SCIENCE

DEBORAH WILKINSON
WAYNE STALLARD

SAGE | Learning Matters

Learning Matters
An imprint of SAGE Publications Ltd
1 Oliver's Yard
55 City Road
London EC1Y 1SP

SAGE Publications Inc.
2455 Teller Road
Thousand Oaks, California 91320

SAGE Publications India Pvt Ltd
B 1/I 1 Mohan Cooperative Industrial Area
Mathura Road
New Delhi 110 044

SAGE Publications Asia-Pacific Pte Ltd
3 Church Street
#10-04 Samsung Hub
Singapore 049483

Editor: Amy Thornton
Senior project editor: Chris Marke
Project management: Swales and Willis Ltd, Exeter, Devon
Marketing manager: Lorna Patkai
Cover design: Wendy Scott
Typeset by: C&M Digitals (P) Ltd, Chennai, India
Printed in the UK

Library of Congress Control Number: 2019944397

British Library Cataloguing in Publication Data

A catalogue record for this book is available from the British Library

ISBN 978-1-5264-7269-4
ISBN 978-1-5264-7270-0 (pbk)

At SAGE we take sustainability seriously. Most of our products are printed in the UK using responsibly sourced papers and boards. When we print overseas we ensure sustainable papers are used as measured by the Egmont grading system. We undertake an annual audit to monitor our sustainability.

CONTENTS

ABOUT THE AUTHORS

Dr Deborah Wilkinson is a qualified primary teacher with over 20 years' experience in education. She is currently a Senior Lecturer in Education at the University of Chichester where she teaches outdoor learning, primary science and Science, Technology, Engineering and Mathematics (STEM). She is interested in how questions are used in primary science lessons and how collaborative action research can support changes in teaching practice.

Wayne Stallard is director of Olive Tree Education and has over 20 years' experience working as a science educator. This experience has enabled him to provide science consultancy services to a range of clients including: government agencies, Science Learning Centres, primary schools, universities (Initial Teacher Training), as well as providing teacher training outside the UK. He is interested in teachers' understanding of the summative assessment in primary science, as assessment of science has always been a great passion.

HOW TO USE THIS BOOK

This book is about the types of evidence that can be used in order to demonstrate whether or not children have 'mastered at greater depth' the primary science curriculum. It is part of every teacher's role to assess children's understanding of science concepts as well as their ability to work scientifically, and many teachers are already getting to grips with demonstrating how their children have 'mastered' the learning outcomes. However, it is time to consider how we evidence if children have truly mastered the learning outcomes, as outlined in the programmes of study in the National Curriculum. This book, therefore, considers the value in providing children with 'rich' learning tasks that will enable them to apply, analyse, evaluate and/or create by using their learning to solve exciting and novel problems. Consequently, the underlying principle of this book is to consider the use of assessment opportunities that can be integrated into units of work to support the teaching and learning cycle as well as providing useful evidence of mastery of skills and knowledge.

Part 1 consists of four chapters that provide the theoretical underpinning linked to the idea of 'mastery at greater depth' in primary science. It is useful to begin by reading these chapters as they will help you to understand the link between effective planning and assessment. In this section there will be opportunities to pause for thought with some learning tasks that will enable you to develop your understanding and link theory and practice together.

Chapter 1 reflects upon how effective learning in science may be realised in order to support children to make progress in their conceptual understanding, as well as developing key skills linked to working scientifically. The chapter presents the importance of providing children with opportunities to engage in different types of enquiry and problem-solving through 'rich' learning tasks so that they have the opportunity to work as scientists. The idea of 'flipping' the learning is also presented.

Chapter 2 builds on the teaching approaches discussed in Chapter 1 but carefully considers the importance of teacher questioning as a tool to support and assess learning. The chapter presents a table of question types that can be applied to the classroom. There is then a consideration of how we can develop children's questioning skills.

Chapter 3 will take a brief look at the theories behind mastery, e.g. Bloom's (1968) Learning for Mastery and Keller's (1968) Personalised System of Instruction. It will then focus on how Learning for Mastery links to formative assessment to evidence mastery of science subject knowledge. The chapter will consider how the National Curriculum currently supports 'mastery' learning. In addition, there will also be an exploration of what is determined as 'good' assessment practice for formative and summative assessment in primary science.

Chapter 4 considers how the principles of mastery can be applied to practice. The links between mastery and planning are considered, such as how the learning objective and success criteria are developed. Practical ways of collecting assessment evidence are also illustrated.

Part 2 begins by considering science in the early years before presenting 'rich' learning tasks that are low-threshold, high-ceiling activities (tasks that *all* children are able to access but challenges the more able, so as to develop their thinking further) in order to provide teachers with assessment information for *all* groups of learners. The tasks link to the programmes of study, as laid out in the National Curriculum and are designed to provide a reliable source of evidence to demonstrate mastery of concepts.

Part 1

THE THEORY BEHIND MASTERY IN PRIMARY SCIENCE

1
THE EFFECTIVE TEACHING OF PRIMARY SCIENCE

CHAPTER OBJECTIVES

This chapter will allow you to achieve the following outcomes:

- have an understanding of the importance of stimulating curiosity through artefacts, visitors to school and visits;
- reflect upon what effective teaching and learning in science entails;
- consider the value of working scientifically through different types of enquiry to ensure progression in skills and knowledge of concepts;
- understand the value of planning for 'rich' learning tasks to ensure an inclusive learning environment is established as well as how to 'flip' the learning during a lesson.

LINKS TO THE TEACHERS' STANDARDS

S1 – set high expectations which inspire, motivate and challenge pupils

S2 – promote good progress and outcomes by pupils

S5 – adapt teaching to respond to the strengths and needs of all pupils

LINKS TO THE NATIONAL CURRICULUM

Key Stage 1 Programme of Study

During years 1 and 2, pupils should be taught to use the following practical scientific methods, processes and skills: observing closely, using simple equipment; performing simple tests; identifying and classifying; using their observations and ideas to suggest answers to questions; gathering and recording data to help in answering questions.

Lower Key Stage 2 Programme of Study

During years 3 and 4, pupils should be taught to use the following practical scientific methods, processes and skills: asking relevant questions and using different types of scientific enquiries to answer them; setting up simple practical enquiries, comparative and fair tests; making systematic and careful observations and, where appropriate, taking accurate measurements and recording findings using simple scientific language, drawings, labelled diagrams, keys, bar charts and tables.

Upper Key Stage 2 Programme of Study

During years 5 and 6, pupils should be taught to use the following practical scientific methods, processes and skills: planning different types of scientific enquiries to answer questions, including recognising and controlling variables where necessary; recording data and results of increasing complexity using scientific diagrams and labels, classification keys, tables, scatter graphs, bar and line graphs; using test results to make predictions to set up further comparative and fair tests.

(DfE, 2014)

INTRODUCTION

In this chapter we begin by considering how we might stimulate children's curiosity in science while focusing on the importance of children working scientifically. The chapter concludes by presenting the types of enquiry that children should have the opportunity to engage in over the duration of an academic year, sequencing the learning and the value of 'rich tasks'.

STIMULATING CURIOSITY

The importance of children actively constructing their knowledge through practical enquiry and discussion is recognised across the world as being an effective way for them to learn science. It is through working scientifically that children can be supported to evaluate their understanding of the world around them. Therefore, teaching science needs to involve more than just subject-knowledge input. Children need to work as scientists and should have the opportunity to test and try out ideas, communicate findings and to evaluate their evidence when drawing conclusions. However, children need to be stimulated to be curious in order to pose questions, undertake investigations, solve problems and answer questions in the first instance.

THE VALUE OF TRIPS AND VISITORS

So, how do we stimulate curiosity? A good starting point is to know what your local community has to offer so that you can consider how these people and resources can be used to enhance science learning. For example, an adult interested in gardening or a person with a science-related job could enhance the curriculum but a parent of a newborn, who is willing to talk to children about the needs of a baby, has much knowledge that can be shared with children in Key Stage 1 when learning about the basic needs of humans for survival. It is worthwhile asking parents and grandparents if they are prepared to share their interests, hobbies (even an activity such as candle-making has useful links to material science) or job with children and plan these into the units of work. STEM ambassadors, local secondary schools, university departments (a music department can provide really engaging input to a unit on sound) and local industries may also be able to support your school. It is also useful to be mindful of national initiatives such as RSPB Birdwatch, RHS Campaign for School Gardening, British Science Week, STEM Projects, The Big Bang, Great Bug Hunt, Eco Schools/Flag, as these all raise the profile of science and stimulate children's curiosity.

Trips do not need to involve expensive coach hire. For example, trips to a local garden centre, an allotment, the local fire station, beach, woodland, supermarket or even a graveyard (great for comparing different types of rock) all enhance experiences for children. Ideally, try to plan for a visit for your class at least twice a year as this will help children to understand how science is relevant to their life and may spark an interest in a future science-related career. When planning trips that involve coach hire, it is useful to think of cross-curricular links so that you can get 'two, or more, for the price of one' because skills and concepts learnt in one subject area can be used to reinforce and support learning in another. For example, scientists and historians both use enquiry skills to further their understanding. Therefore, children may explore an artefact using careful observation, pose questions about its use, consider what it is made from and evaluate whether or not it is the 'best' material using an enquiry (e.g. what is the 'best' material for a drinking vessel and what are the modern equivalents?). As well as linking effectively to material science, the session could also develop children's understanding of continuity and change when learning about history (Wilkinson and Kinoulty, 2018). In this instance, children might consider how different materials have been used over time. It is useful to make yourself a chart of possible contacts and resources, as shown in Figure 1.1 for a unit of work on plants for a Year 1 class.

There is a great deal of content that needs to be taught in the science curriculum (and limited time!) so there is a need to think carefully about how we deliver our lessons. If we are not careful, we could be in danger of planning science lessons that develop a superficial understanding of concepts in order to cover the programmes of study in the National Curriculum. There is, therefore, merit in thinking about how ideas link and using other core subjects to weave more science into the curriculum. In this instance we may consider how we can use mathematics lessons to analyse data or English lessons to communicate findings and to develop language skills.

THE CLASSROOM ENVIRONMENT

In the classroom, consider having an interesting artefact on display (this could be as simple as an acorn that has been deformed by a gall, or a conker still within its case or even a piece of science

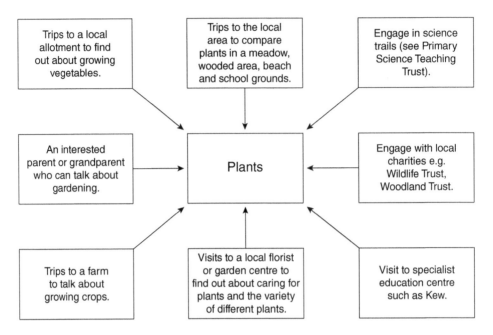

Figure 1.1   Possible ways to enhance children's curiosity about plants

equipment such as a set of Newton metres – children can look closely at the different sized springs and can explore which are best at pushing and pulling different objects). Picture books, story books, poems and non-fiction books linked to the topic may also provide interest and stimulate curiosity. Libraries often put together 'loan boxes' of books linked to a topic area that you can borrow for a term, so it is worth exploring this resource.

Think carefully about your classroom display boards. You may contemplate having a working wall dedicated to science that you develop over the duration of the term, or half term. Consider including 'Wow Words' and posters depicting different types of enquiries (see Figure 1.2) so that children can begin to think about what sort of enquiry is most suited to answer a particular question. Information posters containing facts about the topic area are also a good idea.

We have found that having a large KWHL grid (see Chapter 4) is a good idea, as children can share what they know and would like to find out. Undertaking this activity will enable you to identify misconceptions and may influence how you plan and deliver your lessons. On the KWHL grid there is value in having a place for children to add their questions as well as a space for them to answer them.

To support the development of children's questioning skills you might wish to add some question stems ('How ...', 'Why ...', 'What ...', 'When ...', 'If ...', 'Does ...' etc.) to your science display. Also add some visual prompts and interactive resources and change these as the unit of work progresses. For example, if you are teaching sound you might have some unusual musical instruments on display at the beginning of the unit of work and change these to an object that allows the children to apply their learning of sound by having a balloon which contains a nut (see below in Figure 1.3).

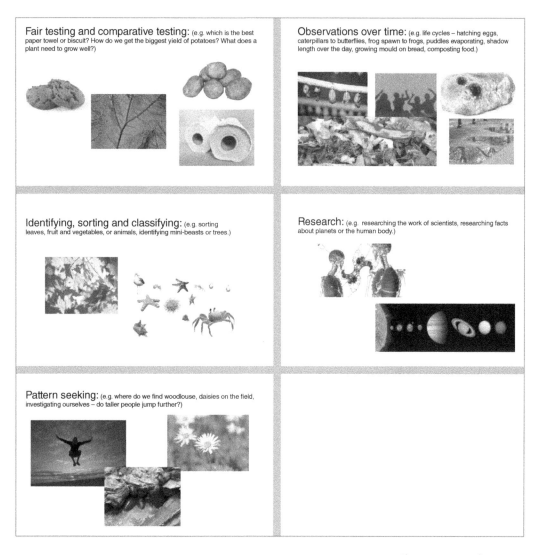

Figure 1.2   Enquiry posters

(Pictures from the posters were sourced from Pixabay: https://pixabay.com/)

In this activity, the sound is made by the corners of the nut hitting the side of the balloon and resulting in a sound – the faster you spin the balloon, the higher the pitch. Children may wish to find out if other objects result in a similar sound.

On your working wall you may decide to have a question of the week. An intriguing question such as *Did you know that you can predict the weather using pine cones?* or *Did you know that nearly all garden snails have their shell 'coils' turning right or spiralling in a clockwise direction?* may stimulate children to find out if these ideas are true. Another approach would be to encourage children to act as a detective to respond to 'I wonder …?' type questions (for example, *I wonder what has been eating the lettuces?*).

Figure 1.3   Balloon stimulus

Initially it might be the teacher asking 'I wonder …' and 'Did you know …?' questions but it is even more valuable if children begin to pose these types of questions themselves. It is important to remember, however, that there should be curriculum time available to enable children to explore things that are of interest to them.

Finally, do not forget to celebrate children's work when they have worked well as a scientist and remember to highlight how and why the work is good so that children can use this as a model for future learning.

LEARNING TASK

Do you currently have a science display – how is it used to raise the profile of science in your classroom?

Think about your science lessons and planning. How do you stimulate children's curiosity?

SCIENCE ENQUIRY

Scientific enquiry encompasses a number of key process skills such as observing, posing questions, making predictions, planning investigations, gathering evidence, interpreting evidence, considering explanations and communicating results and conclusions (Department for Education, 2013). It is important to remember that these skills need to be taught, so careful modelling of these key skills is important, especially during Early Years and Key Stage 1. Independence should be encouraged and children should be given opportunities to make choices when planning the enquiry, selecting resources and deciding how they will interpret, record and communicate their ideas in a variety of ways. Therefore, it is important that children have been exposed to multiple methods of communication such as: writing an advert or news report, composing a song or poem, writing a letter or leaflet, producing a piece of art work, making models, presenting photographs taken of drama or observations, labelled drawings and diagrams, etc. There is a very good app called Science Journal by Google, which is free to download, and can help children to record and present their ideas digitally.

There are also some useful posters entitled 'Working Scientifically in the Primary Classroom: Progression of Enquiry Skills' (see Useful Links at the end of the chapter). These posters could be displayed in the classroom as a reference point when undertaking an investigation and/or put into children's books to use as an assessment tool to ensure progression of skills across the primary curriculum. We have seen an adapted version of these posters used to good effect in a Key Stage 1 setting whereby photographs have been added to the poster when children have displayed a particular skill such as observation or use of language (see Figure 1.4). When adding the photograph to the display, it is important to talk to children about the skills that they have used and celebrate their ability to work scientifically.

For older children the posters can be used to enable them to reflect upon the skills that they have used in the lesson and to put a tick and a date next to those that they feel they have used to good effect in their science lessons. When planning lessons, you might wish to consider focusing upon one type of skill during the lesson. It might be that you want to develop children's recording skills, so this will be the focus. In another lesson, you might wish to focus on communicating findings. Therefore, aligned with a learning objective and success criteria for subject knowledge, you may also wish to plan a learning objective and success criteria for working scientifically.

HOW TO DEVELOP THE SKILL OF OBSERVATION

As mentioned previously, good science learning, in our opinion, begins with ensuring that children are curious, and sitting alongside being curious is the important skill of observation. Children will often want to observe something that is of interest to them, therefore to develop the skill of observation it is important to provide children with interesting items, such as toys. Children will often begin by making 'broad' or 'gross' observations by focusing on the colour, size and shape of the object and may sort and classify according to these criteria. However, if children have time to talk and explore how things work or move, then their observations often become more 'specific' or 'fine' as they can use their knowledge to interpret their observations. As a result, children will be better positioned to notice patterns, similarities and differences. Johnston (2008) argues that observations can be grouped in the following ways:

- Affective – where the child shows interest and is motivated to observe

- Functional – where the child is keen to find out how something works

- Social – interacting, demonstrating and talking about observations

- Exploratory – asking questions and furthering scientific enquiry

It is easy to assume that children will be able to observe, but there is merit in teaching this skill. To encourage children to 'look' carefully, ask them some attention focusing questions, such as:

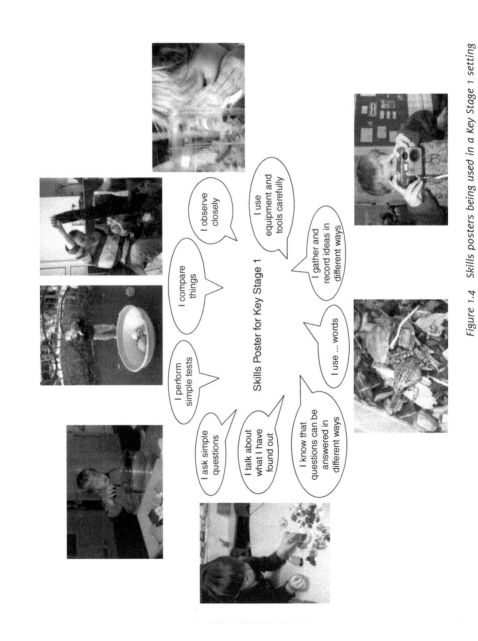

Figure 1.4   Skills posters being used in a Key Stage 1 setting

- What can you see?

- Have you noticed?

- What happens when you …?

- In what ways are they (e.g. seeds, mini-beasts or rocks) similar or different?

- What is the same about these leaves?

- Can you see the lichens growing on the stones?

- Could you tell the difference between the two rocks with your eyes closed?

- What difference do you see when you look at the rocks using a hand lens compared to just using your eyes?

Another good approach to developing observation skills is to encourage children to draw or sketch an item so that they notice key features. In addition to this, you should talk to children about how scientists observe in order to draw make predictions and draw conclusions. For example, if studying habitats, as the teacher, you should ask the children how they might systematically observe mini-beasts, animals or plants in order to make inference about the types of habitat they are best suited to live in.

If you have the space in your classroom, you could consider having a task that encourages children to observe. In Figure 1.5 there are three examples of easy-to-use activities that would encourage children to observe carefully and systematically so that they can begin to make inferences based upon their observations.

Figure 1.5   Tasks to stimulate observation

The first picture shows a 'cloud in a jar'. Shaving foam is added to water and food colouring is slowly added to the shaving foam (cloud). As more food colouring is added, the cloud becomes darker and children will see the colouring go into the water (acting like rain). A way of helping children to understand the water cycle is shown in the second picture – 'water cycle in a bag' – whereby children can clearly see the condensation and precipitation. The third picture uses water and fruit tea-leaves. Children simply observe what happens to the tea-leaves when added to water. We were surprised by the number of questions that children generated when watching these mini-investigations! There is merit in keeping these types of activities on display for a number of weeks so that children can explore their questions.

The Wellcome Trust has developed a free website, Explorify, with activities designed to spark curiosity and develop children's observation skills while supporting their ability to reason and justify (see Useful Links at the end of the chapter). We really liked the Zoom In, Zoom Out tasks, as children have to look very carefully at a magnified image. As an early morning task, you could include pictures from the internet of a magnified image and children have to guess what the object is. Alternatively, the activities can be woven into lessons as a tool to stimulate talk. In our experience children enjoy these tasks and will often want to share their own research with the class.

TYPES OF ENQUIRY

When planning science, it is important that children are not only exposed to fair testing but answer questions using a range of enquiry types. There are five types of enquiry (see Figure 1.2) that are identified in the National Curriculum, and children should have the opportunity to engage in these over the duration of each academic year:

- Observation over time

- Pattern seeking

- Research

- Comparative testing and fair testing

- Identifying, sorting and classifying

(DfE, 2014, p169)

Table 1.1 highlights some examples of the different types of enquiry that Year 1 children may engage in over the duration of the year.

In our experience, there is often a little confusion relating to the use of comparative/fair testing and pattern seeking, so it is useful to consider when you might use pattern seeking, as opposed to fair testing. Comparative or fair testing involves changing one variable while keeping the others the same. For example, when investigating the 'best' material to keep a cup of tea hot, children would change the type of material but would keep the temperature of the water, the cup type and the number of layers of material surrounding the cup of tea the same. It is then possible to measure or observe the effect this has on the temperature of the tea. Pattern seeking is used when there is little, or no control over the variables. For example, when investigating which coloured flowers bees prefer. When measuring, observing and recording natural phenomena it is not always possible to control the variables, so pattern seeking needs to be used. Biological investigations tend to be

Table 1.1   Examples of enquiry types linked to Year 1 science

Type of enquiry	Example
Observation over time	Observed how plants change over the seasons.
Pattern seeking	Explored if taller children jump further.
Research	Researched what animals eat (included correspondence with a zoo keeper or prepared question to ask when visiting a pet shop).
Comparative testing and fair testing	Explored materials to establish the 'best material' for a dog's basket.
Identifying, sorting and classifying	Explored how to group leaves and/or animals.

pattern seeking, e.g. 'does a taller person jump further?' will encourage children to look for patterns and relationships in the data. It would not be classed as fair testing as it not possible to control variables – it is unlikely that an individual will be able to jump in the same way each time as there is often an element of competition!

LEARNING TASK

Map the enquiry types that children in your class engage with over a unit of work (or over the course of the year). Are children experiencing all types of enquiry across the year? Which type of enquiry type are you most confident with?

DEVELOPING MATHEMATICAL SKILLS IN SCIENCE

Once children have decided upon the type of enquiry that is most suitable to answer a question or solve a problem, they then need to consider how they will record, communicate and evaluate their findings. It is easy to assume that children will be able to draw graphs and tables but there is merit in teaching these skills carefully as it is easy to construct them incorrectly.

Starting with tables, it is helpful to talk through with children what the headings will be in terms of 'what we will change' and 'what we will measure'. If you are undertaking an investigation to explore how objects move on different surfaces, you would probably produce a table like the first image on the next page.

After children have been shown this, they can then decide on their own headings for other investigations later in the year. When children have produced a table of results, they may sometimes transfer the data to a graph. Put simply, children can be taught that 'what we changed' goes on the horizontal axis and 'what we measured' goes on the vertical axis (see the second image on the next page).

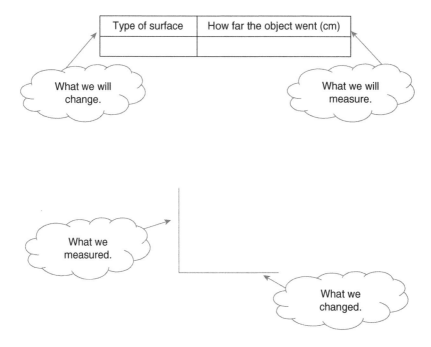

Children may need support in understanding what type of graph to use. A line graph can be used when the variables are described using numbers, whereas bar charts are used when the variables are described using words and numbers. To help comprehend this a little better, you might encourage them to sort enquiry questions into two piles: 'Suitable for a line graph' or 'Suitable for a bar chart' (Goldsworthy and Pouchard, 2008, p10, provide some good sorting activities).

Statements might include the following ideas:

- How does the height of a sunflower change over time? (Line graph)

- How does shadow length change over the course of a day? (Line graph)

- Do people with longer legs jump further? (Line graph)

- Does the type of seed influence the height it will grow over a week? (Bar graph)

- Which is the best material for a ...? (Bar graph)

It is important to remember that the production of a table of results, chart or graph is not the end point in an investigation. Children need to be taught how they can use the graph or chart to draw conclusions and to look for anomalies. This may begin by encouraging children to look for patterns (especially good when focusing on line graphs) and to tell a story about the line graph (Goldsworthy et al., 1999, Activity 1, provides some good examples to use in the classroom). We had fun with the children by providing them with two graphs depicting how quickly two teachers ate a chocolate finger biscuit during break time. Children had to 'tell the story' from the following two graphs shown in Figure 1.6.

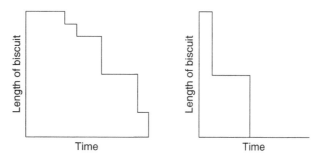

Figure 1.6   Eating chocolate biscuits graph

Sometimes the outcomes to an investigation may not be as expected – however, do not worry about this because this is what science in the real world is like. Scientists do not always know the answer to the outcomes of their investigations. Instead, view this as a learning opportunity to discuss the value of repeated measurements and methods employed. You might even think about the work of scientists and the notion that science progresses by serendipity moments (the work of Fleming is a good case in point in his discovery of penicillin).

RICH TASKS

Presenting children with a rich task or an open-ended challenge is a particularly effective teaching approach to adopt. These challenges or tasks work successfully because they can be *explored at a variety of levels and solved in different ways, allowing all children to participate in the process* (Rickard, 2013, p4). A well-designed rich task can allow for different avenues of exploration, communication and reasoning and does not necessarily have a defined 'end-point'. Indeed, it is identified in the document, Teacher Assessment Framework (science) at the end of Key Stage 2 that *children should be encouraged to raise further questions that could be investigated, based on their data and observations* (DfE, 2018, p6). Therefore, children need to be given time to apply their learning and to reflect upon their practical investigations and to think about new learning. For the learning process to be authentic, children should investigate ideas that they (and sometimes you!) do not know the answers to.

THE LEARNING PIT AND DEVELOPING INDEPENDENCE

The process of enquiry can be a challenge (both for teachers and children). To develop independence and help children to conceptualise how to solve a problem, the Learning Pit Model, as presented by Nottingham in 2017, could be used (see Figure 1.7). The model links well to working scientifically and follows the process of enquiry that should begin by stimulating curiosity.

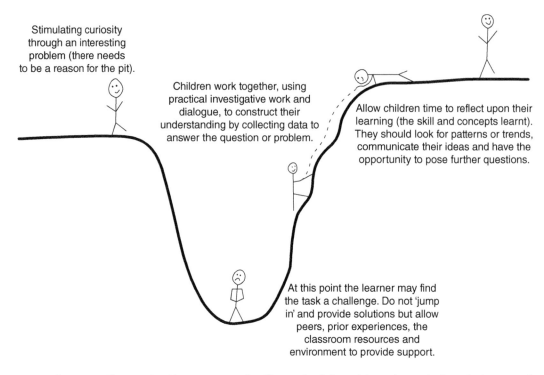

Stimulating curiosity through an interesting problem (there needs to be a reason for the pit).

Children work together, using practical investigative work and dialogue, to construct their understanding by collecting data to answer the question or problem.

Allow children time to reflect upon their learning (the skill and concepts learnt). They should look for patterns or trends, communicate their ideas and have the opportunity to pose further questions.

At this point the learner may find the task a challenge. Do not 'jump in' and provide solutions but allow peers, prior experiences, the classroom resources and environment to provide support.

Figure 1.7 The Learning Pit to support scientific enquiry (adapted from the work of Nottingham, 2017)

It is important to consider how the task is structured in order to support *all* learners in the class. The problem should encourage children to want to 'enter' the pit. This may be achieved by having a relevant, interesting context and could be framed from a child's question. Ideally, the problem should aim to stimulate cognitive conflict so that children will want to check their understanding through practical, hands-on learning. We have found that the use of concept cartoons, designed by Naylor and Keogh (2000) are a particularly useful tool to use in order to rouse cognitive conflict. Other approaches include careful use of teacher questioning so that children's thinking is challenged.

It is useful to remember that the problem needs to be within the child's grasp but in advance of their reasoning. To enhance a deeper level of learning, there is value in children being in the 'bottom of the pit'. In feeling that the task is a challenge, children need to know that it is okay to feel confused and 'stuck', because this is often when learning happens. However, we do not want children to remain at the bottom of the pit – they will need to get out eventually!

To help children 'climb out of the pit', we can consider the place of social constructivism. In order to provide 'challenge', children should be working in the zone of proximal development, which is the zone between what a learner can do or understand without assistance and what they can do with assistance (Vygotsky, 1978). The 'assistance' could be in the form of feedback, modelling of ideas, explaining, questioning, classroom displays and posters and task structuring. The support may be provided by the teacher or peers (just be mindful that peers may have naive ideas, so listen in to conversations carefully and be prepared to challenge thinking). It is important to note that science lessons provide children with ample opportunities to work with others to form and clarify ideas, assess their own understanding, to negotiate choices, use and apply their skills, listen to each other and to reflect upon responses of others.

THE VALUE OF TALK FOR LEARNING

Talk is conducive to learning because talking helps children to clarify their thinking and develops their reasoning skills which, according to Dawes (2004), provides a powerful stimulus for learning. Therefore, talking and understanding can be assumed to be inherently social and integral to learning. Indeed, Vygotsky (1978) argues that higher-ordered thinking happens first in a social plane through social interactions and talk and later in an intrapersonal plane (inside the learner's head).

Figure 1.8 Posters to structure children's thinking

(Pictures from the posters were sourced from Pixabay: https://pixabay.com/)

This highlights the importance of co-participation between the child and yourself (or another child) and the value of dialogue while negotiating the zone of proximal development (the zone between what a learner can do or understand without assistance and what they can do with assistance).

DEVELOPING A SUPPORTIVE CLASSROOM ENVIRONMENT

In order to establish a supportive classroom environment, whereby children can be more autonomous and independent, you might consider using posters. These should be designed to provide some scaffolding to help children begin their 'climb out' of the Learning Pit (see Figure 1.8).

THE IMPORTANCE OF REFLECTION

It is important that time is made available for children to reflect upon their learning when working on an enquiry. A Reflective Spinner (see Figure 1.9, developed from a question spinner idea by Goldsworthy, 2011) could be used in pairs or table groups so that children think about how they

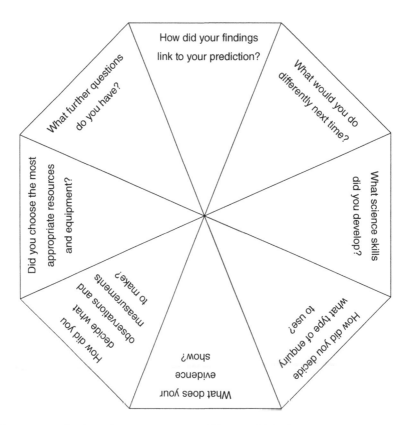

Figure 1.9 Reflective Spinner to encourage children to think about their learning during an enquiry.

have worked as scientists and developed their skills of working scientifically. The idea is to use a paperclip at the centre of the spinner, put the tip of a pencil through the paperclip and flick the paperclip; the paperclip is the pointer and will indicate which question should be answered and reflected upon.

A NOTE ABOUT INCLUSION

As teachers, we are required to provide an inclusive learning environment so that all children can make progress. We would argue that delivering science in the way described throughout this chapter ensures that the learning is inclusive due to the practical and collaborative nature of the lessons. Indeed, you may observe that children who find mathematics and writing a challenge, may be very good at problem-solving. In addition, sometimes the more able children may feel very uncomfortable when being challenged and may need their peers for support. It is, however, useful to consider how children with English as an additional language, or children with special educational needs and disability, may be supported to use their scientific language accurately so you might pre-teach the meaning of scientific words. For example, there is much technical vocabulary that can be used to describe the properties of a material, such as 'flexible' or 'brittle', that may be new vocabulary. Therefore, giving children time to touch a range of materials that are flexible and teaching the word 'brittle' can allow children the opportunity to understand the link between materials and scientific language (Wilkinson and Stallard, 2017).

SEQUENCING A LESSON

The decisions you make about how a concept is introduced, and the planned activities, play a crucial role in determining how children will participate during lessons. Instead of presenting children with 'facts', during the input of the lesson it is possible to 'flip' the learning. In this instance, the lesson begins with an authentic problem that the children need to solve (using one of the five types of enquiry covered earlier in this chapter) and at the end of the lesson the teacher provides the subject-knowledge input to ensure that children have understood key scientific concepts. In this way, the teaching includes both authoritative (directly showing, explaining and modelling ideas) and problem-solving (through working scientifically) teaching approaches. Scott and Ametller (2007) argue that if children have been told about a science concept via an authoritative approach, then time should be available during the lesson for children to enquire. By using both authoritative and practical approaches, the teacher is able to intervene, classify and 'bridge the gap' between student knowledge and the accepted scientific view of phenomena. This way of working will help children learn science concepts rather than just remembering the practical activity.

Another way of 'flipping the learning' may be realised by providing some of the subject-knowledge input as a home learning task. You may decide to use the school's virtual learning environment to upload a video or game so that children can develop their understanding of topics being taught. This would then 'free up' curriculum time so that children can engage at a deeper level of understanding through problem-solving tasks and enquiries, as they will already have developed their science subject-knowledge base.

┌─── **CHAPTER SUMMARY** ───

This chapter explored the importance of stimulating curiosity as a starting point for the effective teaching and learning of primary science. In doing so, there was a consideration of how the classroom environment, trips and learning from 'experts' within the school community can raise the profile of science. This followed with a discussion of how to present children with problems to solve, via different types of enquiry. Solving problems is acknowledged as being a challenge for many children but when undertaken correctly, can support the development of children's conceptual knowledge, as well as their skills of working as scientists. The 'Learning Pit' along with posters, and a Reflective Spinner, are presented as 'tools' to scaffold thinking so that children develop their resilience and independence. This section followed by considering the importance of inclusive practice, and how children with English as an Additional Language (EAL) can better access the curriculum. The chapter concluded by exploring the value in 'flipping' the learning so that curriculum time can be released for applied learning.

┌─── **USEFUL LINKS** ───

Explorify at: https://explorify.wellcome.ac.uk/

Developing global links at: globaldimension.org.uk/support/school-links-partnerships/

Working Scientifically in the Primary Classroom: Progression of Enquiry Skills can be accessed at: www.ciec.org.uk/pdfs/primary/working-scientifically.pdf

STEM Ambassadors at: www.stem.org.uk/stem-ambassadors

Woodland Trust at: www.woodlandtrust.org.uk/

Primary Science Teaching Trust at: https://pstt.org.uk/

REFERENCES

Dawes, L (2004) Talk and learning in science classrooms. *International Journal of Science Education*, 6(6): 677–95.

Department for Education (2013) *The National Curriculum in England: Framework Document*. London: DfE.

Department for Education (2018) Teacher assessment frameworks at the end of key stage 2. Available at: www.gov.uk/government/publications/teacher-assessment-frameworks-at-the-end-of-key-stage-2 [Accessed July 2018].

DfE (2014) *The National Curriculum in England: Framework Document*. London: DfE. Available at: https://assets.publishing.service.gov.uk/government/uploads/system/uploads/attachment_data/file/381344/Master_final_national_curriculum_28_Nov.pdf [Accessed 3 January 2019].

Goldsworthy, A (2011) Effective questions, in Harlen, W (2011) *ASE Guide to Primary Science Education.* Hatfield: ASE.

Goldsworthy, A and Pouchaud, B (2008) *Science Enquiry Games: Active Ways to Learn and Revise Science Enquiry Skills.* Stafford: Millgate House.

Goldsworthy, A, Watson, R and Wood-Robinson, V (1999) *Getting to Grips with Graphs from Bar Charts to Lines of Best Fit.* Hatfield: ASE.

Johnston, J (2008) What does the skill of observation look like in young children? *Paper presented at BERA Annual Conference, Heriot-Watt University, Edinburgh*, 3–6 September 2008. Available at: www. leeds.ac.uk/educol/documents/174237.pdf

Naylor, S and Keogh, B (2000) *Concept Cartoon in Science Education.* Stafford: Millgate House.

Nottingham, J (2017) *The Learning Challenge: How to Guide Your Students Through the Learning Pit to Achieve Deeper Understanding.* Thousand Oaks, CA: Corwin Teaching Essentials.

Rickard, C (2013) *Essential Primary Mathematics.* Milton Keynes: Open University Press.

Scott, P and Ametller, J (2007) Teaching science in a meaningful way: Striking a balance between 'opening up' and 'closing down' classroom talk. *School Science Review, 88*(324): 77–83.

Vygotsky, LS (1978) *Mind in Society: The Development of Higher Psychological Processes.* Cambridge, MA: Harvard University Press.

Wilkinson, D and Kinoulty, M (2018) Two for the price of one. *Primary Science, 152*: 5–7.

Wilkinson, D and Stallard, W (2017) Materials – what's the matter? *Primary Science, 150*: 5–7.

2

THE IMPORTANCE OF QUESTIONS IN PRIMARY SCIENCE

CHAPTER OBJECTIVES

This chapter will allow you to achieve the following outcomes:

- have an understanding regarding the place and value of questions in science lessons;
- consider how different questions can be asked to support learning;
- know how to support children in raising their own questions during science lessons.

LINKS TO THE TEACHERS' STANDARDS

S2 - promote good progress and outcomes by pupils

S6 - make accurate and productive use of assessment

LINKS TO THE NATIONAL CURRICULUM

Key Stage 1 Programme of Study

Asking simple questions and recognising that they can be answered in different ways.

(Continued)

(Continued)

Lower Key Stage 2 Programme of Study

Asking relevant questions and using different types of scientific enquiries to answer them.

Using results to draw simple conclusions, make predictions for new values, suggest improvements and raise further questions.

Identifying differences, similarities or changes related to simple scientific ideas and processes.

Using straightforward scientific evidence to answer questions or to support their findings.

Upper Key Stage 2 Programme of Study

Planning different types of scientific enquiries to answer questions.

(DfE, 2014)

INTRODUCTION

This chapter begins by considering the value of questions in primary science lessons. Most primary school teachers would list questioning as one of the key ways in which they influence children's learning. Questioning is a key feature of scientific enquiry and of teaching science, and asking questions serves as one of the fundamental modes of communication between teacher and child. Questioning is commonly employed for a wide variety of purposes, such as keeping children actively involved in learning, assessing understanding or identifying naive ideas, facilitating thought, evaluating and monitoring progress as well as serving as a behaviour management tool. The way in which you question children is dependent on a number of variables, and these will be explored in this chapter. To support you in increasing your repertoire of questions over the duration of a lesson, a table of question types is presented. Following on from considering the value of teacher questions, the chapter then explores why children should be supported to ask and answer their own questions. Again, a table of question types that children may ask is presented. The chapter concludes by modelling how children's questions may be answered via an investigation.

TEACHER QUESTIONING

Your understanding of subject specific pedagogy may determine the way in which you plan and execute your science lessons. Alexander (2008) asserts that when teachers aim to simply 'impart knowledge' this does little to promote the skills of reasoning in children. In a teacher-centred approach, where the aim is to 'transfer knowledge' in a transmission–reception model, this ensures that children are passive in their learning. Questioning in this teaching approach often follows a certain pattern of interaction: the teacher asks a question, the children respond and the teacher evaluates the answer (Alexander, 2008). Lemke (1990) terms this pattern of teacher–student–teacher interaction as 'triadic dialogue', otherwise known as Initiation-Response-Evaluation (IRE). In this model the teacher is the authority of knowledge and tests and evaluates whether children have been successful in verbalising the taught knowledge. It can be assumed that it is only the teacher who asks the questions and knows the answers. It could also be argued that IRE tends to restrict deeper, reflective thinking and can alter the way in which children behave in lessons. When children feel that they have provided the answer they tend not to think of alternative answers or viewpoints.

An alternative approach proposed by Scott and Ameteller (2007) is to use the Initiation-Response-Feedback-Response-Feedback chain (IRFRF), which results in more interactive and collaborative learning as the teacher poses a question, the child responds and the teacher then directs the turn back to the class without evaluating the answer provided. We like to think of this as being a bit like a game of table tennis: serve a question to a child (avoid 'hands-up' in order to ensure that all children know that they may be asked to respond and engage) then 'bat' the question to another child (even a third) before making a comment or responding to their answers. It is important that you provide children with time to formulate an answer. Budd-Rowe (1986) identified that teachers should provide children with at least three seconds to answer an open-ended question as they need to decipher the meaning of the question before generating a response. We suggest that you say a rhyme in your head prior to responding/rephrasing or bouncing the question to another child. 'One, two, three, four, got to wait a little more' (Wiliams, 2016), and there will be pronounced changes in the responses provided. By employing the IRFRF chain, children can engage with each other's ideas and problem-solving approaches.

THE ROLE OF THE TEACHER

It can be a challenge to move from the teacher-centred approach and towards a more learner-focused approach in order to make the learning experience more engaging. A range of issues, such as limited teaching time, resourcing issues and sometimes the teacher's confidence with some aspects of subject knowledge impact upon how a teacher questions and organises their science lessons. If teachers do not feel confident with one or more of these variables, this may result in teachers using more teacher-centred methods. Figure 2.1 shows the variables that influence teaching choices.

The role that the teacher adopts during enquiry learning is crucial if children are to learn the scientifically accepted ideas of science, and for Posner *et al.* (1982) the teacher as a clarifier of ideas or presenter of information is not adequate for helping children accommodate new concepts. Therefore, instead of monitoring the lesson by telling children how to undertake an investigation, checking that children are 'on task' and directing the learning (often by using closed questions and classroom-management questions), there is merit in sometimes acting as a 'fellow investigator' or experienced co-learner, guide or co-inquirer (Martin, 2006). In this role, genuine problems (that you, as a teacher may not know the answers to) are presented and the teacher and pupils work together to investigate. This allows the teacher to think through their ideas so that reasoning skills are modelled to the children. This may be perceived as a breath of fresh air as teachers can sometimes learn alongside the children and do not have to have all of the answers!

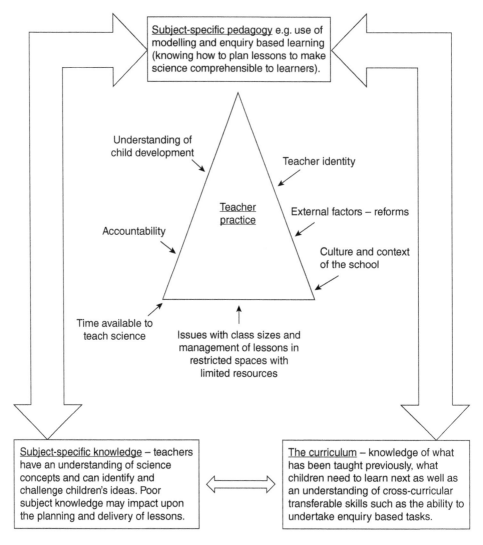

Figure 2.1 The interplay between variables that impact upon teaching approaches employed in science

QUESTION TYPES

The type of questions that teachers pose during lessons influences the level of thinking operations that children engage in (Chin, 2002). Chin, Brown and Bruce (2002) assert that teachers can support children to think more critically and creatively by being aware of different question types, and then using them during teaching episodes. Table 2.1 shows the different type of questions that can be asked during science lessons, as well as their functions.

Table 2.1   Question types and their function in science lessons

Question type	Description	Example
Closed	Often requires a one-word answer and is used to check for understanding or recall of facts.	*How many bones in the body?* *So you mean ...?* *What is ...?*
Open	Requires a more open response in the form of a sentence or explanation. There is more than one possible answer.	*What do you think might happen if ...?* *Can you tell the class about ...?* *So what does that have to do with ...?* *What do you think may happen if ...?*
Person-centred and opinion questions	Questions that include the pronoun 'you'. The question provides limited jeopardy on the part of the learner.	*So what do you think the problem is?* *Why do you think it ...?* *What is your opinion?*
Active	Questions support children in being active in order to find the answer to questions. Involves questions that lead to some sort of investigative work.	*What do you think might happen?* *How would you test ...?* *What do you notice ...?* *How many/how long?* *What if ...?* *Can you find a way to ...?* *If ... then ...?* *How do you think that may have happened?* *Can you see a pattern?* *What evidence do you have?* *What did we learn about ... today?*
Comparison	Questions require children to use careful observation skills in order to answer a question. Could also be used in a plenary to compare findings.	*In what ways are they the same/ different?*
Application	Supports children in applying their conceptual understanding to another situation.	*Can you find a way to ...?* *How would you use ...?* *How would you apply what you have learned to develop ...?*
Defining questions	Asks for clarification.	*What do you mean ...?* *Can you give me an example of...?* *Could you explain how ... happens?* *Are you sure?* *Do you mean that ...?* *So ...?* *In other words ...?* *Tell me more about ...?* *Why ...?* *How ...?*

OPEN/CLOSED AND PERSON-CENTRED QUESTIONS

All questions can be classified as open or closed. Although closed questions tend to be perceived as being 'negative', they have their place in a lesson. Closed questions are effective when recapping on prior learning and checking pupils' knowledge, and are particularly valuable if science is only being taught once a week. Open questions require more expansive answers and encourage children to share their thoughts and opinions. These questions require children to formulate one or more sentences as an answer.

Questions can also be considered from an emotional viewpoint. Indeed, Harlen and Qualter (2014) categorised teacher questioning into two distinct categories: 'person-centred' and 'subject-centred' questioning. Person-centred questions are regarded as supportive and use the pronoun 'you'. Asking a child 'What do *you* think?' or 'Why do *you* think that?' to probe thinking provides limited jeopardy on the part of the child in that they might provide an incorrect answer; it is asking children what they think, rather than trying to guess what is in the teacher's head and trying to provide the 'right answer' (Carin *et al.*, 2005). According to Harlen (2000), person-centred questions are a useful tool to find out what children know, whereas subject-centred questions are often closed and reintroduce an element of 'right and wrong'.

ACTIVE QUESTIONS AND THE LINK TO WORKING SCIENTIFICALLY

Active questions are useful to ask when children are undertaking practical work because they are designed to develop the skills of working scientifically by encouraging children to think about what they might observe, predict, record, test and evaluate. Comparison questions link well to active questions and support the process of observation (very good if working on sorting and classification tasks), but can also be used to good effect to enable children to compare their findings. If children have undertaken similar investigations but have different solutions, it is useful to pause and to think about why the findings and conclusions are different.

Defining questions can be asked at any point during a science lesson. These questions ask for clarification and encourage children to provide a more expansive answer. Asking 'why' or 'how' questions 'probes' thinking and encourages more analysis. It is a useful technique to ask a question and to pause before responding (or bouncing the question to another child) as this will encourage the child to provide a more expansive answer. Sometimes, you might add the word 'because', 'and', 'so' or the phrase 'tell me more' to indicate to the child that you would like to know more about their thinking.

To take the learning further, application questions are valuable in encouraging children to think about how their learning from an enquiry might be applied to other concepts.

LEARNING TASK

Digitally record the input to your lesson and use the table to analyse the types of questions that you ask. Do you pose more open or closed questions? Is there a way in which you can ask a wider range of questions, e.g. developing observational skills by asking comparative questions?

WHY CHILDREN SHOULD RAISE THEIR OWN QUESTIONS

Being able to ask questions and have the opportunity to answer them is fundamental to active and meaningful science enquiry work (Chin, 2006). The formulation of a question that deepens understanding is considered to be a creative act at the heart of what science is all about (Chin, 2007). Child-generated questions can serve different functions for learners, such as confirmation of expectations as well as helping them to problem-solve and develop their knowledge base (Biddulph *et al.*, 1986). Chin (2002) asserts that question generation is an important cognitive strategy as it focuses the learner's attention on the main ideas and content of the lesson, and plays a significant role in learning. Therefore, being able to pose questions enables the learner to make sense of the world, to construct meaning, help to scaffold ideas, explore concepts and advance understanding (Chin, 2007).

The value of child-generated questions in science has been emphasised in research as they serve to fill a recognised knowledge gap and thus extend knowledge. In order to close the knowledge gap, teachers need to listen carefully to the questions that children ask as these will serve to guide the teacher in understanding what children have been thinking about, their current conceptual understanding, their misconceptions, their reasoning as well as what they want to know. Where classroom conditions are 'safe', children will ask a range of questions, from the curious to those which reveal 'troubled thinking'.

COGNITIVE DEMAND OF CHILDREN'S QUESTIONS

Chin (2004) asserts that the level of thinking required of children influences the kind of questions that they ask, and thus how active they will be in their learning. When assigned tasks that require instructions and step-by-step procedures, children are not engaged at high cognitive levels. As a result, children will be more inclined to ask procedural or management questions to make sure they do things correctly and in accordance with teacher expectations (Chin, 2004). Conversely, problem-solving activities engage children in conversations at a higher level and deep-thinking questions may be asked. Questions asked in response to curious items often support children to predict what might happen and result in a cascade of enquiry and procedural work. It could be surmised that unless children are stimulated to be curious, they will not ask questions at the higher cognitive demand level.

A main reason for children's questions being posed in lessons, according to Watts *et al.* (1997), is when learners find the content and context of the lesson confusing because they do not understand what is being said by the teacher or their peers. The confusion on the part of the learner ensures that they will need to ask for clarification in order to make sense of what is being said (Lemke, 1990). However, when there is a need for clarification of an idea or scientific concept, the questioning may take place silently, in the learner's mind, rather than out loud. Here, the child is reflecting upon their learning by asking themselves questions to help them to monitor their own understanding. During this phase they engage in an internal dialogue as they look for patterns and connections as well as establishing relationships with their prior learning (Chin, 2004). If children are not verbalising their thinking, then teachers may have a compromised understanding of the cognitive conflicts that lie behind the learner's confusion (Lemke, 1990). The questions that children pose are indicative of a child's understanding:

By posing questions, pupils are shaping and exposing their thoughts and hence opportunities will be provided for teachers to have some insight into children's thinking and conceptual understanding. Questions asked by children can lead teachers towards making appropriate assessments of children's understanding or alternatively their misconceptions.

(Woodward, 1992, p16)

Woodward (1992) asserts that the type of questions asked by children provides teachers with an understanding of conceptual understanding or confusion that learners may be experiencing. This enables the teacher to plan for learning opportunities in order to address the naive idea or confusion.

LEARNING TASK

How and when are children in your class supported to ask their own questions?

QUESTIONS CHILDREN ASK

Just as teacher questions have been presented in various taxonomies of question types, so have children's questions. Table 2.2 shows the types of questions that children may ask during science lessons.

Table 2.2   Children's questions

Question types and examples of questions	Function of question
Basic information questions What does the dictionary say about salt? What does the sachet contain?	To generate questions in response to cues or to seek information.
Wonderment What would happen if ...?	Application of an idea – requires children to be active and to test an idea.
Philosophical questions I wonder why that happens if ...?	Does not require another person to answer; just a think-out-loud question.
Procedural or management questions Who would like to count? What do we do next?	Requires clarification of a procedure or task. Children negotiating roles during experimental work.
Comparison questions Which goes fastest? In what ways are they the same/different?	Use of observational skills to compare variables.
Explanatory and exploration questions Why does the sachet float?	Children needing an explanation based upon their observation of events that they have observed or items they have been exploring.

Children should be supported in asking 'what if …', 'why does …' and 'how would …' type questions to ensure deeper thinking ensues rather than simple recall type questions ('what is …?'). The 'what if?' questions help students to explore possibilities and to consider alternatives and test relationships, whereas the 'why?' type questions stimulate children to think about cause-and-effect relationships. Teaching categories of questions may support children in understanding that different types of questions elicit different thinking processes and that answers can be derived in different ways.

SUPPORTING CHILDREN TO ASK AND ANSWER THEIR OWN QUESTIONS

So, where to begin! The starting point in developing children's questioning skills is to encourage them to raise any kind of question because to indicate too soon that science is concerned with certain types of questions might deter children from raising their own (Harlen and Elstgeest, 1992). However, Chin (2002) found that when teachers begin to apply question-production strategies with students, the result is the generation of a large proportion of factual questions as these are easier to generate, so be prepared for these and value them. However, becoming aware that some kinds of questions can be answered by enquiry-based learning, is a point of progress. Once this is understood, then children can be supported in rephrasing vague questions into a form that can be investigated (Harlen and Elstgeest, 1992). Alternatively, think carefully about how the lesson is introduced – is it open-ended and does it allow children time to explore and raise questions from an interesting hook?

In order to illustrate the link between a good hook, question-generation and enquiry work, find an idea that sparks curiosity and can be answered in different ways. One of our favourite inputs involved a lesson on biscuits. At the beginning of the lesson children were shown a video clip, downloaded from YouTube, 'The spy who loved cookies'. In the clip the 'Cookie Crown' had been stolen and was about to be dunked in the 'Cookie Dunker of Doom' by Lady Finger. The children agreed that it was unlikely that the Cookie Monster would save the crown, so a new one would need to be made. Children were subsequently encouraged to 'explore' different types of biscuit (which is hardest, most crumbly, can be dunked the most times?). At this point there is merit in asking some comparative-type questions and/or attention-focusing questions to support children's observations. After 'exploring' the biscuits, ask children to think about questions relating to biscuits; you might like to provide children with the following question stems:

- Do/does …?

- Is/are …?

- How …?

- Can …?

- What …?

- What happens when …?

The questions were written on sticky notes and added to enquiry posters in order to help children begin to understand how their questions may be investigated, as shown in Figure 2.2.

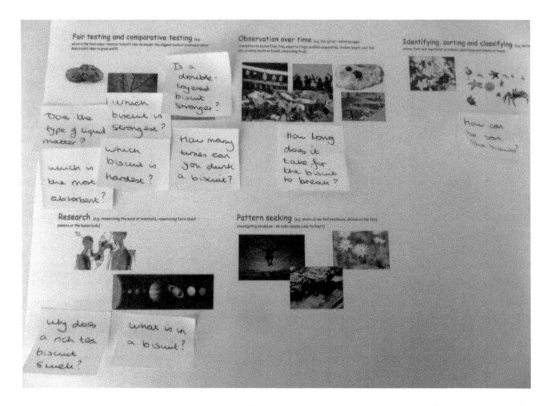

Figure 2.2   Questions generated from a hook and exploration

The questions were then used to find an answer to the question 'Which is the "Best" biscuit to remake the Cookie Crown?' The use of the word 'best' enabled children to have ownership over their learning (e.g. determining what they mean by 'best') and children worked on different ideas. Therefore, children had the opportunity to select their own equipment and were supported to present their data in the most appropriate way. During the plenary there was some dispute about which biscuit would be 'best' and children had the opportunity to question and challenge their peers.

LEARNING TASK

What sort of questions do children in your class ask? How are these valued and shared?

┌─ **CHAPTER SUMMARY** ─────────────────────────────┐

This chapter began by considering the reasons teachers ask questions, along with barriers that may impede them from employing learner-centred teaching approaches. If teachers do not feel confident with their subject knowledge, understand progression, have limited comprehension of subject pedagogy, along with issues of limited resources and curriculum time, they may be inclined to ask more closed questions and not provide children with the opportunities to ask and answer their own questions. A table of question types that teachers can adopt was then shared, so that when planning lessons, a range of question types can be considered. The chapter then focused on why children ask questions, and the question types that they ask. The chapter concluded by presenting an approach to develop children's questioning skills.

└───┘

┌─ **USEFUL LINKS** ────────────────────────────────┐

De Bono, E (1985) *Six Thinking Hats*. Boston, MA: Little, Brown and Company (shows practical ways to help children to ask questions and to think more deeply).

Explorify at: https://explorify.wellcome.ac.uk/ (provides good questions that stimulates thinking in response to an activity).

Wilkinson, D (2016) The use of questions in primary science: A collaborative action research study. University of Southampton, School of Education, Doctoral thesis.

└───┘

REFERENCES

Alexander, R (2008) Culture, dialogue and learning: Notes on an emerging pedagogy, in Mercer, N and Hodgkinson, S (eds) *Exploring Talk in School*. London: Sage.

Biddulph, F, Symington, D and Osborne, R (1986) The place of children's questions in primary science education. *Research in Science and Technological Education*, 4(1): 77–88.

Budd-Rowe, M (1986) Wait time: Slowing down may be a way of speeding up! *Journal of Teacher Education*, 37: 43–50.

Carin, AA, Bass, JE and Conant, TL (2005) *Teaching Science as Inquiry* (10th Ed). Upper Saddle River, NJ: Prentice Hall.

Chin, C (2002) Student-generated questions: Encouraging inquisitive minds in learning science. *Teaching and Learning*, 23(1): 59–77.

Chin, C (2004) Questioning students in ways that encourage thinking. *Teaching Science, 50*(4): 16–21.

Chin, C (2006) Classroom interaction in science: Teacher questioning and feedback to students' responses. *International Journal of Science Education*, 28(11): 1315–346

Chin, C (2007) Teacher questioning in science classrooms: Approaches that stimulate productive thinking. *Journal of Research in Science Teaching*, 44(6): 815–43.

Chin, C, Brown, DE and Bruce, BC (2002) Student-generated questions: A meaningful aspect of learning in science. *International Journal of Science Education, 24*(5): 521–49.

DfE (2014) *The National Curriculum in England: Framework Document*. London: DfE. Available at: https://assets.publishing.service.gov.uk/government/uploads/system/uploads/attachment_data/file/381344/Master_final_national_curriculum_28_Nov.pdf [Accessed 3 January 2019].

Harlen, W (2000) *Teaching, Learning and Assessing Science 5–12* (3rd Ed). London: Sage.

Harlen, W and Elstgeest, J (1992) *Unesco Sourcebook for Science in the Primary School*. Available at: www.arvindguptatoys.com/arvindgupta/unescoprimary.pdf [Accessed 2018].

Harlen, W and Qualter, A. (2018) *The Teaching of Science in Primary Schools* (7th Ed). London: David Fulton.

Lemke, JL (1990) *Talking Science: Language, Learning and Values*. Westport, CT: Ablex.

Martin, DJ (2006) *Elementary Science Methods: A Constructivist Approach* (3rd Ed). Independence, KY: Wadsworth Cengage Learning.

Posner, GJ, Strike, KA, Hewson, PW and Gertzog, WA (1982) Accommodation of a scientific conception: Toward a theory of conceptual change. *Science Education, 66*(2): 211–227.

Scott, P and Ameteller, J (2007) Teaching science in a meaningful way: Striking a balance between 'opening up' and 'closing down' classroom talk. *School Science Review, 88*(324): 77–83.

Watts, M, Gould, G and Alsop, S (1997) Questions of understanding: Categorising pupils' questions in science. *School Science Review, 79*(286): 57–63.

Wiliams, D (2016) Content then process: Teacher learning communities in the service of formative assessment. Available at: www.youtube.com/watch?v=TMBsTw37eaE

Woodward, C (1992) Raising and answering questions in primary science: Some considerations. *Evaluation and Research in Education, 6*: 15–21.

3
MASTERY IN PRIMARY SCIENCE

┌─────────────── **CHAPTER OBJECTIVES** ───────────────┐

This chapter will allow you to achieve the following outcomes:

- have a developing understanding of the theories that support 'mastery learning';
- begin to understand what 'mastery' might look like in primary science;
- consider the role assessment plays in supporting and evidencing 'mastery learning'.

└──┘

┌─────────── **LINKS TO THE TEACHERS' STANDARDS** ───────────┐

S1 – set high expectations which inspire, motivate and challenge pupils

S2 – promote good progress and outcomes by pupils

S5 – adapt teaching to respond to the strengths and needs of all pupils

S6 – make accurate and productive use of assessment

└──┘

┌─────────── **LINKS TO THE NATIONAL CURRICULUM** ───────────┐

The programmes of study describe a sequence of knowledge and concepts. While it is important that pupils make progress, it is also vitally important that they develop secure understanding of each key block of knowledge and concepts in order to progress to the next stage. Insecure,

(Continued)

└──┘

(Continued)

superficial understanding will not allow genuine progression: pupils may struggle at key points of transition (such as between primary and secondary school), build up serious misconceptions, and/or have significant difficulties in understanding higher-order content.

(DfE, 2014, p168)

INTRODUCTION

In this chapter we will begin by exploring the theory behind the term 'mastery'. 'Mastery' is used by many teachers when discussing primary mathematics so we will consider how this might relate to the primary science curriculum. There will then be a discussion about how formative and summative assessment links to teaching and learning and evidence of learning. Finally, we will explore what is considered 'best practice' in assessment of primary science and how this might support the process of evidencing mastery learning.

MASTERY

The first thing to consider when discussing 'mastery learning' is that it is not a new concept in education. Kulik *et al.* (1990, p265) explain that there were a number of individualised systems developed in the United States of America (USA) in the 1920s and 1930s, but it was not until the 1960s that it became more prominent in the USA education system. In 2013, the English National Curriculum was revised and the term 'mastery' was made explicit, particularly in mathematics. This is because the mathematics curriculum in England is based on mathematic curriculums from countries that perform highly in international league tables and these curriculums all include aspects of mastery (NCETM, 2014; Morgan, 2017). The mathematics curriculum in the UK is based on the idea that children who grasp concepts quickly are challenged through greater depth learning and 'rich tasks', rather than being introduced to new content. This led the authors of this book to ask the questions: 'What is mastery?' and 'How could it be applied to the primary science curriculum?'

THEORY UNDERPINNING 'MASTERY'

When considering mastery there are two influential approaches; Bloom's Learning for Mastery and Keller's Personalised System of Instructions (Kulik *et al.*, 1990, p265). Keller's (1968) Personalised System of Instructions (PSI) was developed to enable pupils to learn without an instructor/ teacher being continuously present (Eyre, 2007). The system relies heavily on the use of text or other media, which breaks learning into smaller steps so that pupils can engage with the content. When a pupil feels that they have 'mastered' the unit they undertake a test. If they pass the test they move on to the next unit; if they do not pass the test they have to re-engage with the unit materials and try again. The system does not penalise the pupil for having to take the test multiple times. The system could be likened to the theory part of the driving test in the United Kingdom, where the individual reviews the theory and then undertakes a test to check the level of mastery. Therefore, given unlimited time and an individual's belief and/or drive to want to master a topic, theoretically any topic could be mastered. However, as the current National Curriculum sets out key goals that must be mastered in a fixed time period, this approach may not enable all children to reach mastery.

Bloom's (1968) Learning for Mastery (LfM) is better suited to the English education system/ classrooms as it considers the importance of both the teacher and the learner in ensuring the learner achieves mastery in a given time period. Although Bloom is usually the person credited with this approach to learning, he actually adapted the work of Carroll (1963, cited in Bloom, 1968) by demonstrating how the five elements (first identified by Carroll) could be applied during the teaching process (Zimmerman and Dibenedetto, 2008).

The five elements are listed in Table 3.1.

Table 3.1   Table to show the five elements of Mastery for Learning adapted from Bloom 1968

Elements of LfM	Description
Aptitude for particular kinds of learning	*Aptitude is the amount of time required by the learner to obtain mastery of a learning task* (Carroll, 1963, cited in Bloom, 1968, p3).
	Given that curriculum time is 'fixed' in most schools by the school timetables, it can be assumed that some children will have insufficient time to master the learning. However, Bloom (1968) claimed that over 90 per cent of children can achieve mastery. Therefore, it could be argued that in this group some will achieve mastery much more quickly and they may be able to demonstrate mastery at a deeper level.
Quality of instruction	*Quality of instruction in terms of the degree to which the presentation, explanation, and ordering of elements of the task to be learned approach the optimum for a given learner* (Carroll, 1963, cited in Bloom, 1968, p4).
	Therefore, if the teacher does nothing to differentiate the quality of instruction, then few children will be able to achieve mastery. It is important to consider aspects such as length of initial input (e.g. do all children need the same length or content of input?); scaffolding (e.g. what support might be needed at different points in the lesson? Is the same support needed for all children?); depth of mastery (e.g. how will those children who achieve mastery quickly be enabled to develop greater depth?).
Ability to understand instruction	*Ability of the learner to understand the nature of the task he is to learn and the procedure he is to follow in the learning of the task* (Carroll, 1963, cited in Bloom, 1968, p5).
	Primarily this focuses on the learner's ability in basic skills such as being able to read and comprehend; verbally communicate; ability to work as a member of a team and/or independently; apply simple mathematics skills. This is also closely linked to the quality of instruction, e.g. how does the teacher remove barriers to learning/understanding of instruction?

(Continued)

Table 3.1 (Continued)

Elements of LfM	Description
Perseverance	*Perseverance is the time the learner is willing to spend in learning* (Carroll, 1963, cited in Bloom, 1968, p6).
	This is an aspect that many schools in England are developing with their children through the work of Dweck's theory of 'Growth Mindsets'. This is a key element because if the individual's perseverance is less than the time required for them to achieve mastery then it is unlikely they will master the learning. Therefore, the task has to be pitched just right. If it appears too difficult this could impact on the individual's willingness to persevere, and equally if it is too easy.
Time allowed for learning	*The time spent on learning is the key to mastery* (Carroll, 1963, cited in Bloom, 1968, p7).
	Time allowed for learning needs to at least match the time the learner needs to obtain mastery, otherwise it is unlikely the learner will achieve mastery. However, as discussed earlier, the timetable for learning objectives for curriculum subjects is already set, and therefore there may be insufficient time allocated to develop mastery. Therefore, the teacher may need to consider making the 'learning steps' smaller in order to give the learner sufficient time to master the learning in each lesson.

When looking at Table 3.1 it can be easy to see why each of these elements have to be considered and planned for if mastery for learning is to be achieved. Mastery of mathematics draws on Bloom's Mastery for Learning but also incorporates Bruner's theory for the concrete – pictorial – abstract pedagogy (Morgan, 2017). It could be argued that Bruner's pedagogy is equally as valid in the teaching and learning in science. After all, children need to experience phenomena first-hand to truly begin to understand, and/or question, if they are to develop a deep understanding or mastery of science concepts.

LEARNING TASK

Consider the last science lesson you taught:

- What adaptions did you make to take into account the five elements of LfM?
- Are some elements easier to consider/plan for than others? If so, why are they harder? What do you need to develop in order to ensure you include all aspects?
- Did the lesson also include Bruner's theory (concrete, pictorial and abstract)? If so, which of these aspects were present?
- Can you think of science activities which would illustrate Bruner's theory?

WHAT MASTERY MEANS FOR PRIMARY SCIENCE

Now that the theory of mastery learning has been briefly explored, it is important to consider what 'mastery learning' in primary science means. Bloom (1968) explains that it is important to first consider what mastery of the subject looks like, as without this how is it possible to tell whether an individual has mastered the subject (for teachers in England the mastery of curriculum subjects has already been decided in the attainment objectives identified in the National Curriculum)? There are clear expectations of what the children should have mastered in science (both in terms of subject knowledge and 'Working Scientifically') by the end of Key Stage 1 and Key Stage 2. However, as discussed previously (in Table 3.1) some children, in our opinion, should have the opportunity to achieve 'mastery at a greater depth'.

Bloom (1956, cited in Krathwohl, 2002) originally identified six cognitive domains, as identified in Figure 3.1, which were later updated to better match the skills needed by twenty-first-century learners, as shown in Figure 3.2 (Anderson and Krathwohl, 2001).

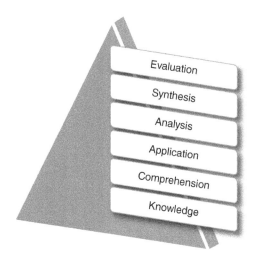

Figure 3.1   Bloom's (1956) taxonomy of educational objectives

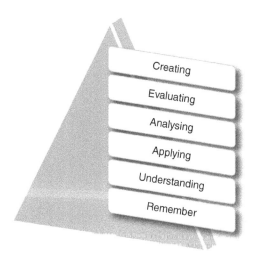

Figure 3.2   Bloom's revised taxonomy of educational objectives (Anderson and Krathwohl, 2001)

Anderson and Krathwohl (2001, pp67–8) define these domains as:

- **Creating**: Putting elements together to form a coherent or functional whole; recognising elements into a new pattern of structure through generating, planning or producing.

- **Evaluating**: Making judgements based on criteria and standards through checking and critiquing.

- **Analysing**: Breaking materials into constituent parts, determining how these parts relate to one another and to an overall structure or purpose through differentiating, organising and attributing.

- **Applying**: Carrying out or using a procedure through executing or implementing.

- **Understanding**: Constructing meaning from oral, written and graphic messages through interpreting, exemplifying, classifying, summarising, inferring, comparing and explaining.

- **Remembering**: Retrieving, recognising and recalling relevant knowledge from long-term memory.

These domains go from simple cognitive demand (remembering) to complex cognitive demand (creating). Therefore, these domains can be used when considering what 'mastery at greater depth' might look like in any curriculum subject. When reviewing the current National Curriculum for Primary Science (DfE, 2013a), it is clear that mastery is set around the domains of 'understanding' and 'applying'. Therefore, if individuals are going to be able to demonstrate mastery at greater depth, teachers need to provide opportunities for these individuals to apply, analyse, evaluate and/or create while still learning the same content as the other children in the class. It is in Part 2 of this book that we will give examples of how this might be achieved.

So how is mastery implemented into the lesson? In order to better understand this, it would be first useful to know a little about assessment, including the history, principles and what is currently considered as best practice, in the National Curriculum, as assessment plays a key role in helping individuals first achieve mastery and then enabling some to achieve mastery at a greater depth. In addition, it can also hinder the ability to deliver a mastery curriculum.

ASSESSMENT

A BRIEF HISTORY OF ASSESSMENT IN THE PRIMARY NATIONAL CURRICULUM FOR ENGLAND

Prior to the introduction of the National Curriculum for England in 1988 there was no *national system of statutory testing* and the government had *no control of the primary curriculum* (Wyse and Torrance, 2009, p213). Instead, the local authorities (LAs) had responsibility for the curriculum and the monitoring of summative assessment outcomes undertaken in their schools (Black *et al.*, 2010). However, due to the growing 'dissatisfaction' of industry leaders, who expressed concern that school leavers did not have the skills they needed (Whetton, 2009, p138; Wyse and Torrance, 2009), the National Curriculum was introduced by an Act of Parliament in 1988 for children aged between 5 and 16 years of age.

In order to ensure the British taxpayer was getting *value for money in terms of the national investment of education* (Wyse and Torrance, 2009, p215) the government wanted to develop national statutory assessments in order to monitor improvements in education. To achieve this, an assessment group was formed (Task Group in Assessment and Testing – TGAT) and made recommendations to the government, including: using a wide range of assessment methods and tasks; teacher involvement in class-based assessment; moderation of test results; and assessments following a single set of procedures (Wyse and Torrance, 2009, p215). TGAT made these recommendations as they believed a wide evidence base, using work from the classroom, would create valid assessments, and moderation would ensure reliability. Having a single set of procedures for assessment would reduce the workload on teachers, as once they had mastered it for one subject they could apply it to other curriculum subjects too. However, the government did not fully implement these recommendations (Black *et al.*, 2010; Wyse and Torrance, 2009). The Standard Assessment Tasks (SATs) were developed between the late 1980s and early 1990s for Key Stage 1 and these involved a mixture of centralised tests and teacher assessment for English, mathematics and science. However, the SATs tested a much narrower domain of each core subject than would have been achieved by the TGAT recommendation but they were cheaper to produce (Black and Wiliam, 2010). This is an important point to note as it led to education professionals questioning the validity of the tests (Whetton, 2009). In 1994 the Key Stage 2 SATs were introduced, but unlike the Key Stage 1 SATs these only involved centralised written tests and did not require teacher assessments (ibid.).

The SATs enabled the government to focus on its aim of accountability and produce league tables to compare schools in terms of their outcomes for children. The use of national testing for accountability purposes is not uncommon for governments across the Organisation for Economic Co-operation and Development (OECD) countries (Connolly *et al.*, 2012; Looney, 2011). Looney (2011) explains that many OECD countries use international league tables to develop their educational policies (as seen in the current National Curriculum, especially with regards to mathematics). However, some countries such as Canada, the United States of America and England incorporate sanctions (e.g. restructuring or closure of a school and dismissal of teaching staff) as a result of accountability data (Harlen, 2013; Looney, 2011). Linking sanctions to the outcome of assessments created 'high stakes' assessment (Black *et al.*, 2010; Looney, 2011; Taras, 2008). High-stakes assessment impacted on the curriculum as teachers 'taught to the tests', in order to achieve better outcomes, and by doing so this resulted in a narrowed curriculum for their children (Abrahams *et al.*, 2013; Black *et al.*, 2010; Collins *et al.*, 2009; Harlen, 2007; Harlen, 2013; Murphy *et al.*, 2013). For primary science, especially at the end of Key Stage 2 (Year 6), this meant that children often only experienced subject knowledge input at the expense of practical investigations, as these skills could not be easily tested by the SATs (Abrahams *et al.*, 2013; Collins *et al.*, 2009). Another unwanted consequence was the impact on the children (e.g. anxiety causing children to not want to go to school during the testing period because of the pressure teachers were under to improve performance/outcomes).

In 2007, the General Teaching Council brought an end to SATs in primary science and teachers have been responsible for reporting on children's attainment through teacher assessment (although the government still tests a random sample of schools to gain a national picture of the health of primary science (Collins *et al.*, 2009; Davies *et al.*, 2014; Earle, 2014). While the removal of the primary science SATs has been largely welcomed by teachers, it has had unintended consequences. This has resulted in primary science becoming a 'poor relation' of the core subjects in the National Curriculum, with Wilshaw (2016) stating:

> *While the vast majority of schools were spending 4 hours or more each week teaching English and mathematics, none devoted a similar time to teaching science, the third core subject on the primary curriculum. Around two thirds indicated that they spent between 1 and 2 hours a week on science teaching. However, for around a fifth of the schools, less than an hour was given to learning the subject.*

There are two important points to consider here with regard to mastery learning in science. The current National Curriculum (DfE, 2013b) is based on mastery learning, and the requirement for teachers is to report on whether the child has met or not met the end of Key Stage requirements (DfE, 2013b). Therefore, given current workload concerns, do teachers need to evidence mastery beyond 'understanding and applying'? We would argue that it is every child's right to be supported and challenged in their learning so that they can achieve what they are truly capable of. This links closely to a number of the current Teachers' Standards (DfE, 2011) – TS 2: Promote good progress and outcomes by pupils; TS 5: Adapt teaching to respond to the strengths and needs of all pupils; and TS 6: Make accurate and productive use of assessment. Therefore, it could be argued that if teachers are not considering 'mastery at a greater depth' in science then they cannot be fully meeting the Teachers' Standards.

The second point to consider is 'time allowed for learning'. As discussed earlier, if there is insufficient time given to the science curriculum and this is less than the time needed for an individual to reach mastery (aptitude), then it is unlikely they will be able to demonstrate mastery. Influence over time allocated for curriculum subjects may be beyond the control of a teacher, but it is something that senior leaders need to consider if they truly want to embrace mastery learning. However, because there are still high-stakes assessment in English and mathematics this may drive the curriculum design in some schools and therefore lead to science and other curriculum subjects being given insufficient time. There may be some hope for those wishing to readdress this balance, as Ofsted inspections currently review the breadth of the curriculum provided and the quality of learning across the range of curriculum subjects.

PRINCIPLES OF ASSESSMENT

When considering the principles of assessment, the first thing that needs to be explored is the function or purpose of assessment.

Looney (2011, p11) simplifies assessment into three categories: *accountability, school and system improvement, and supporting learning.* However, Harlen *et al.* (2015) and Harrison and Howard (2010) challenge this and state that assessment only has two purposes. to improve learning through feedback or to keep track of the learner's progress. The difference here seems to be a philosophical debate about what the true educational purpose of assessment should be; which is to enable the learner to reach their full potential. Harlen *et al.* (2015) and Harrison and Howard's (2010) purposes of assessment would also certainly support mastery learning because it focuses mainly on supporting the learning of the individual. However, given the impact of high-stakes assessment, as discussed earlier, it may be impossible for the class teacher to focus solely on these purposes.

Once the purpose has been established, it is important to consider the process of assessment. The process of assessment for formative (improving learning through feedback) and summative (keeping track of the learner's progress) assessment are the same (Harlen, 2013; Taras, 2005; Taras, 2009; Wiliam, 2000). Figure 3.3 shows the process.

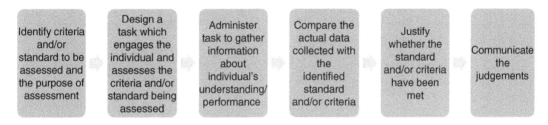

Figure 3.3 *Process of assessment to improve learning through feedback or keep track of a learner's progress (adapted from Harlen, 2005a; Harlen, 2013, p7; Taras, 2009, p58)*

This process has been developed for primary science through the 'Teacher Assessment in Primary Science' (TAPS) pyramid (see link at the end of the chapter). The TAPS pyramid clearly shows that teachers need to plan for assessment, including how evidence of learning in science will be gathered through a range of activities. Once the evidence has been gathered and judgements moderated, it needs to be communicated according to the purpose of the assessment, e.g. feedback to the child (formative assessment) or reporting to parents, the next teacher, the next school, etc. (summative assessment).

The simple diagram (Figure 3.3) represents the process as a linear one, but in reality it is far more complex. For example, at the 'designing a task stage' (e.g. illustrate depth of mastery), there would be a cyclical review happening as the assessor would need to ensure the task or test enables the individual to demonstrate the identified criteria and or standard(s) (e.g. applying, analysing, evaluating and/or creating). The task or test would need to be trialled and modified in light of the information gathered in order to ensure it was fit for purpose, although in reality this does not happen in the classroom because of the demands on teachers' subject, and pedagogical subject, knowledge (Black *et al.*, 2010; Shulman, 1986). In addition, the assessment process might happen once at the end of a unit of work or several times during a lesson depending on whether it is a formative or summative assessment. The process is illustrated by Kolb's (1984) Experiential Learning Cycle (Figure 3.4).

FORMATIVE ASSESSMENT

It is useful to explore what is defined as formative assessment. Several authors (Dunn and Mulvenon, 2009; Looney, 2011; Newton, 2007; Taras, 2005; Wiliam, 2000) all cite Bloom *et al.*

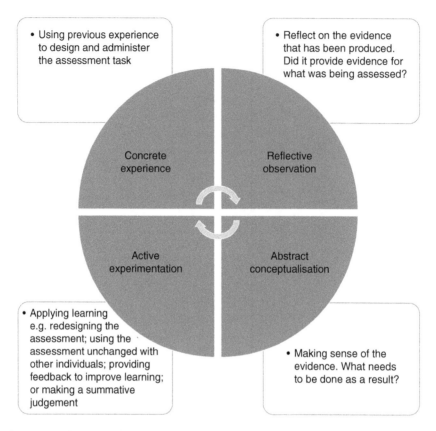

Figure 3.4 Diagram to show Kolb's Experiential Learning Cycle in relation to the assessment process

(1971) and later Sadler (1989) as developing the term formative assessment. Bloom *et al.* (1971, p61) define formative assessment as:

> *The main purpose of formative observations is to determine the degree of mastery of a given learning task and to pinpoint the part of the task not mastered. ... The purpose is not to grade or certify the learner; it is to help both the learner and the teacher focus upon particular learning necessary for movement towards mastery.*

As can be seen in this definition, formative assessment focuses on the smaller steps in learning in order to secure mastery of 'the big ideas' (Harlen *et al.*, 2015). There is no attempt made to award a mark or grade to the learning but to ensure both teacher and pupil are focused on moving the learning forward. This definition has been added to by Sadler (1989, p120) to explicitly identify the role of feedback in formative assessment as it enables the *student's competence by short-circuiting the randomness and inefficiency of trial-and-error learning.* This links directly with the learning theories of Vygotsky's Zone of Proximal Development. The teacher is the 'more knowledgeable other' who helps the child redirect their efforts by giving them feedback to narrow the gap between their current performance and the desired goal.

Figure 3.5 demonstrates how this assessment supports mastery in learning, where Zimmerman and Dibenedetto expect 80 per cent to achieve mastery although this is less than the 90 per cent or more that is claimed by Bloom (1986).

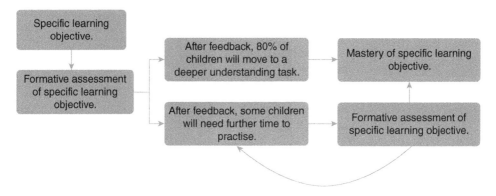

Figure 3.5   A flow diagram of mastery learning test and adaptive instructions (adapted from Zimmerman and Dibenedetto, 2008, p209)

Figure 3.5 demonstrates the mastery process, which begins with the teacher identifying what specific objectives have to be covered in the unit. For the English National Curriculum this has already been identified in the attainment objectives for each subject and topic area. At this point teachers usually undertake some pre-assessment (Guskey, 2010) or cold tasks, to determine what knowledge, skills and understanding the children already have. In some schools this is referred to as a 'cold task' which could take many forms, e.g. teacher questioning, test, activity encouraging children to discuss unit etc. The key purpose of this is to measure the aptitude of individuals, e.g. who might achieve mastery quickly as they already have knowledge to support learning in the new unit (see Chapter 4 for examples of cold tasks).

Next comes the instruction for what will be learnt in the lesson but it is important to remember that in this National Curriculum all children should be learning the same concepts, so the introduction needs to be sufficient (and differentiated) to enable all children to achieve mastery at understanding and/or applying. Either during this instruction or when the children have begun the task, the teacher undertakes further formative assessment to see if individuals are on track to achieve mastery. It is at this point that Figure 3.6 explains the two paths a teacher might take. However, this is where the authors believe that for each lesson there is a third path to be taken (Figure 3.6). This links back to Chapter 1, where flipped learning is discussed and the authors explore the idea of not always telling children concepts.

Figure 3.6 shows that at the formative assessment point, one of three paths can be directed by the teacher. The first is that the formative assessment demonstrates the individual has mastered the objectives and will move straight to the rich task which will enable them to demonstrate depth of mastery. The second pathway is selected if the formative assessment demonstrates the individual

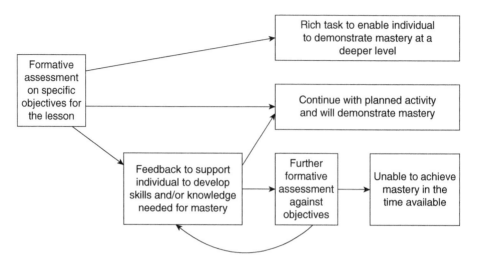

Figure 3.6   A flow diagram of mastery learning test and adaptive instructions (adapted from Zimmerman and Dibenedetto, 2008, p209)

will meet mastery in the time available. The final pathway is used where the formative assessment demonstrates the individual has insufficient ability to meet mastery in the time available, so feedback is provided to help improve this. At this point the individual may go on to achieve mastery at the end of the lesson or may require additional feedback. It is possible that the individual is unable to achieve mastery in the time available. Although formative assessment is only highlighted at key points in the flow diagram, it has to happen continuously as the teacher will want to ensure those they believe will achieve mastery, and/or mastery at greater depth, do in fact achieve this in the time available. These individuals may require additional feedback to ensure this happens.

So what might this formative assessment look like? Research has shown that formative assessment seems to be well embedded in primary science, although some teachers confuse it with more frequent summative assessment as they miss out the feedback element (Black *et al.*, 2003; Earle, 2014). Hodgson (2010) reviewed formative assessment techniques used in primary science which can be seen in Table 3.2.

This evidence was based on a review of 39 research articles from across the *UK primarily, but also extending to Australia, New Zealand, the Asian Pacific Rim and the USA* from 1997 to 2008 (Hodgson and Pyle, 2010, p3). It is difficult to determine how widely this was embedded practice in England as their methodology only explained that the evidence was largely qualitative and not quantitative. There was another study which focused on assessment in primary science undertaken by Earle (2014). She reviewed 91 school submissions for the 'Primary Science Quality Mark' award (PSQM). Again, it is difficult to know how widely these are being used by schools across the UK as the PSQM award requires schools to review and reflect on science assessment (both formative and summative). However, what is interesting is there are similarities between the practice identified in Earle's research and the previous research.

Table 3.2 *Table showing formative assessment techniques in primary science against overarching themes (adapted from Hodgson, 2010, pp15–16)*

Misconceptions and classroom climate	Talk and discussion	Questioning	Feedback	Self and peer assessment
• Concept cartoons • Puppets • Learning journals • Group work • Suspending judgement when thought processes are explained • Teacher values ideas and does not dismiss them	• Presenting ideas in a variety of ways • Highlighting key language in science • Enable pupils time to talk	• Big or rich questions • Model good questions • Keep returning to questions • Using materials to stimulate questions • Providing 'wait time' • No hands up	• Pupil to teacher • Teacher to pupil • Comments against defined criteria • No grades	• Planned for • Self-marking against criteria • Concept maps

---

LEARNING TASK

What methods have you used, or have you seen used, to collect formative assessment in primary science? Are any of these methods used in other curriculum subjects? How is this formative assessment used to support mastery of primary science?

SUMMATIVE ASSESSMENT

Unlike formative assessment, summative assessment in primary science seems to lack the breadth of methods used to collect evidence which is essential if a pupil is to evidence mastery. As with formative assessment there would appear to be general consensus regarding the definition of summative assessment with several authors (Dunn and Mulvenon, 2009; Looney, 2011; Newton, 2007; Taras, 2009; Wiliam, 2000) all citing Scriven (1967, pp2–3) as the source of the definition.

The activity consists simply in the gathering and combining of performance data with a weighted set of goal scales to yield either comparative or numerical ratings.

It can be seen from the quotation that there is a need to gather a range of performance data and compare this against set criteria in order to make a judgement (comparative or numerical). In education this is undertaken at a given point in time (e.g. end of unit of work, term or year) in order to identity the child's achievements (Dunn and Mulvenon, 2009; Hallen, 2005a; Taras, 2005). As the judgement is made usually at the end of learning it is often referred to as 'Assessment of Learning'

(Black and William, 1989 cited in Earle, 2014). Summative assessment seems to be linked mainly with timing in this definition and there is little consideration of the differences regarding the purpose. After all, formative assessment without feedback to the individual is not formative but just summative assessment.

There are two types of summative assessment usually seen in education – external and internal (Harlen, 2005b). External summative assessments are set and usually marked centrally (e.g. SATs). As previously discussed, the type of assessment can have many purposes, e.g. used by parents in deciding which school they would like to send their child to; local authorities to identify schools in need of support; and Ofsted as part of their risk-analysis inspection process. All of which could have a significant impact on the school and the teachers who work within it. Internal summative assessments are usually set by the school or teachers within the school. They are also marked within the school and the information is used to track individual or cohort progress in learning key concepts across the year. This information is also used to report to parents at key points in the year regarding their child's learning. These assessments, although not as high stake, can sometimes be used in teachers' performance management targets, although with the current curriculum these purposes have expanded to include the purposes of external summative assessment.

As part of the review of 91 schools PSQM submissions, Earle (2014) identified the following methods being used for summative assessment. As previously discussed with regard to formative assessment, it is difficult to determine how common these methods are across schools in England. However, one thing that is noticeable is the common use of tests for summative purposes. What is less obvious is the use of any of the formative methods identified in Table 3.2. Given that the process of assessment is the same for summative and formative assessment (Harlen, 2013; Taras, 2005; Taras, 2009; Wiliam, 2000) it is interesting that these teachers are not using formative assessment techniques for summative assessments.

Earle (2014, p217) argues that teachers do not understand what 'good' assessment in science is and therefore, this makes it difficult to improve practice. This is compounded because there is no 'central direction'; schools make up their own systems or buy into commercially produced solutions. The demands of designing summative assessment relies heavily on teachers' subject knowledge and pedagogical content knowledge (Black et al., 2010; Shulman, 1986) and it is clear from the review of assessment in the National Curriculum that teachers have had limited opportunities to develop this. Alternatively, it could be because teachers do not perceive summative and formative assessment as being linked (Dunn and Mulvenon, 2009; Harlen, 2005a; Taras, 2008), which could be because summative assessment is seen as being 'bad' (Harlen et al., 2015; Lau, 2016) and formative assessment is the 'antiseptic' (Taras, 2008, p174).

Harlen et al. (2015) argues that for summative assessment to be effective it should enable children to demonstrate their mastery through a variety of ways. Therefore, tests might be one aspect of demonstrating knowledge and understanding, but there should be others. It is also possible to use evidence gathering for formative assessment purposes to make summative judgements. Harlen et al. (2015) explains that this can be achieved by using 'detailed indicators' (the small steps or 'small ideas' which are set as learning objectives in individual lessons) and the 'coarse-grained criteria' (the National Curriculum learning objectives ('big ideas') (Harlen, 2005b)). An example linked to 'Working Scientifically' is illustrated in Table 3.3.

Table 3.3   An example of how the detailed indicators could provide evidence for the coarse-grained criteria

'Detailed indicators' (Formative assessment criteria)	'Coarse-grained criteria' (Summative assessment criteria)
• Has knowledge and understanding of the five types of scientific enquiry. • Is able to select an appropriate type of enquiry for a variety of questions, justifying choice. • Is able to ask appropriate and productive scientific questions which can be investigated. • Able to explain how to carry out the different experiments and identify which variable will be controlled or changed (where appropriate).	• Planning different types of scientific enquiries to answer questions, including recognising and controlling variables where necessary (DfE, 2013a).

It is important to use multiple sources of information to ensure the individual has mastered the learning and can apply it in a variety of contexts in order to achieve the 'coarse-grained criteria' (Harlen, 2005a).

LEARNING TASK

What methods have you used, or have you seen used, to collect summative assessment in primary science? Are any of these methods used in other curriculum subjects? How is this summative assessment used to support mastery in primary science? Is it based on a broad range of evidence which enables the children to demonstrate their mastery in a range of different ways?

CHAPTER SUMMARY

This chapter has demonstrated that it is possible to achieve mastery in primary science beyond meeting the National Curriculum learning objectives. However, in order for this to happen teachers must consider and provide opportunities for the five elements of LfM (aptitude for particular kinds of learning; quality of instruction; ability to understand instruction; perseverance; and time allowed for learning) but some of these may be beyond their control (e.g. time for learning). In addition, teachers must also use assessment efficiently and effectively to identify those individuals who need help to achieve mastery and provide feedback to support this, as well as identifying those individuals who could achieve mastery at greater depth. For those individuals who have the ability to achieve mastery at a greater depth, teachers will need to consider how they can develop activities which cover the same learning objective (as those who are aiming for mastery) but enable these individuals to demonstrate deeper learning through applying, analysing, evaluating and/or creating.

```
┌─────────────── USEFUL LINKS ───────────────┐
│                                              │
│  Teacher Assessment in Primary Science (TAPS) at: https://pstt.org.uk/resources/curriculum-  │
│  materials/assessment                        │
│                                              │
└──────────────────────────────────────────────┘
```

REFERENCES

Abrahams, I, Reiss, MJ and Sharpe, RM (2013) The assessment of practical work in school science. *Studies in Science Education*, 49(2): 209–51.

Anderson, L and Krathwohl, D (eds) (2001) *A Taxonomy for Learning, Teaching and Assessing: A Revision of Bloom's Taxonomy of Educational Objectives* (complete edition). New York: Longman.

Black, P and Wiliam, D (2010) Inside the black box: Raising standards through classroom assessment. *Phi Delta Kappan*, 92(1): 81–90.

Black, P, Harrison, C, Lee, C, Marshall, B and William, D (2003) Formative and summative assessment: Can they serve learning together. *AERA Chicago*, 23: 1–17.

Black, P, Harrison, C, Hodgen, J, Marshall, B and Serret, N (2010) Validity in teachers' summative assessments. *Assessment in Education: Principles, Policy & Practice*, 17(2): 215–32.

Bloom, B (1968) Learning for mastery. *Instruction and Curriculum. Regional Education Laboratory for the Carolinas and Virginia*. Topical Papers and Reprints, Number 1. Available at: https://files.eric.ed.gov/fulltext/ED053419.pdf

Bloom, BS, Hastings, JT and Madaus, GF (1971) *Handbook on Formative and Summative Evaluation of Student Learning*. New York: McGraw-Hill.

Collins, S, Reiss, M and Stobart, G (2009) The effects of national testing in science at Key Stage 2 in England and Wales. *Education in Science*, 231: 14–15.

Connolly, S, Klenowski, V and Wyatt-Smith, CM (2012) Moderation and consistency of teacher judgement: Teachers' views. *British Educational Research Journal*, 38(4): 593–614.

Davies, D, Collier, C, Earle, S, Howe, A and McMahon, K (2014) Approaches to science assessment in English primary schools (full report, teachers' summary and executive summary). Bristol: Primary Science Teaching Trust.

DfE (2011) *Teachers' Standards*. [Online]. Available at: www.gov.uk/government/publications/teachers-standards [Accessed 1 February 2018].

DfE (2013a) *National Curriculum*. [Online]. Available at: www.gov.uk/government/collections/national-curriculum [Accessed 1 February 2018].

DfE (2013b) *National Curriculum and Assessment: Information for Schools*. [Online]. Available at: www.gov.uk/government/publications/national-curriculum-and-assessment-information-for-schools [Accessed 1 February 2018].

DfE (2014) *The National Curriculum in England. Framework Document*. London: DfE. Available at: https://assets.publishing.service.gov.uk/government/uploads/system/uploads/attachment_data/file/381344/Master_final_national_curriculum_28_Nov.pdf [Accessed 3 January 2019].

Dunn, KE and Mulvenon, SW (2009) A critical review of research on formative assessment: The limited scientific evidence of the impact of formative assessment in education. *Practical Assessment, Research & Evaluation, 14*(7): 1–11.

Earle, S (2014) Formative and summative assessment of science in English primary schools: Evidence from the Primary Science Quality Mark. *Research in Science & Technological Education, 32*(2): 216–28.

Eyre, H (2007) Keller's personalized system of instruction: Was it a fleeting fancy or is there a revival on the horizon? *The Behavior Analyst Today, 8*(3): 317–24.

Guskey, T (2010) Lessons of mastery learning. *Educational Leadership: Interventions That Work, 68*(2): 52–7.

Harlen, W (2005a) Formative and summative assessment: A harmonious relationship? [Online]. *ASF Seminar, 2*: 27.

Harlen, W (2005b) Teachers' summative practices and assessment for learning: Tensions and synergies. *Curriculum Journal, 16*(2): 207–23.

Harlen, W (2007) Primary Review Interim Reports: Research Studies 3/4. *The Quality of Learning: Assessment Alternatives for Primary Education*. University of Cambridge.

Harlen, W (2013) *Assessment & Inquiry-Based Science Education: Issues in Policy and Practice*. Trieste, Italy: Global Network of Science Academies.

Harlen, W, Bell, D, Devés, R, Dyasi, H, Fernández de la Garza, G, Léna, P, Millar, R, Reiss, M, Rowell, P and Yu, W (2015) *Working with Big Ideas of Science Education*. In W. Harlen (ed): Science Education Programme (SEP) of IAP.

Harrison, C and Howard, S (2010) Issues in primary assessment. *Primary Science, 115*: 5–7.

Hodgson, C (2010) Assessment for learning in science: What works well? *Primary Science, 115*: 14–16.

Hodgson, C and Pyle, K (2010) *A Literature Review of Assessment for Learning in Science*. Slough: National Foundation for Educational Research (NFER).

Kolb, DA (1984) *Experiential Learning: Experience as the Source of Learning and Development*. London: Prentice-Hall.

Krathwohl, D (2002) A revision of Bloom's taxonomy: An overview. *Theory into Practice, 41*(4): 212–18.

Kulik, C, Kulik, J and Bangert-Drowns, R (1990) Effectiveness of mastery learning programs: A meta-analysis. *Review of Educational Research, 60*(2): 265–99.

Lau, AMS (2016) 'Formative good, summative bad?' A review of the dichotomy in assessment literature. *Journal of Further and Higher Education, 40*(4): 509–25.

Looney, JW (2011) Integrating formative and summative assessment: Progress toward a seamless system? *OECD Education Working Papers, No. 58*. OECD Publishing (NJ1).

Morgan, C (2017) From policy to practice: Discourses of mastery and ability in England. University College London Institute of Education.

Murphy, C, Lundy, L, Emerson, L and Kerr, K (2013) Children's perceptions of primary science assessment in England and Wales. *British Educational Research Journal, 39*(3): 585–606.

NCETM (2014) Mastery approaches to mathematics and the new national curriculum. National Centre for Excellence in the Teaching of Mathematics.

Newton, PE (2007) Clarifying the purposes of educational assessment. *Assessment in Education, 14*(2): 149–70.

Sadler, DR (1989) Formative assessment and the design of instructional systems. *Instructional Science,* *18*(2): 119–44.

Scriven, MS (1967) The methodology of evaluation (perspectives of curriculum evaluation, and AERA monograph series on curriculum evaluation, no. 1). Chicago, IL: Rand NcNally.

Shulman, LS (1986) Those who understand: Knowledge growth in teaching. *Educational Researcher,* *15*(2): 4–14.

Taras, M (2005) Assessment – summative and formative – some theoretical reflections. *British Journal of Educational Studies, 53*(4): 466–78.

Taras, M (2008) Summative and formative assessment: Perceptions and realities. *Active Learning in Higher Education, 9*(2): 172–92.

Taras, M (2009) Summative assessment: The missing link for formative assessment. *Journal of Further and Higher Education, 33*(1): 57–69.

Whetton, C (2009) A brief history of a testing time: National curriculum assessment in England 1989–2008. *Educational Research, 51*(2): 137–59.

Wiliam, D (2000) Integrating formative and summative functions of assessment. Paper presented to Working Group 10 of the International Congress on Mathematics Education, Makuhari, Tokyo, August 2000.

Wilshaw, M (2016) HMCI's commentary: Science and foreign languages in primary school. [Online]. Available at: www.gov.uk/government/speeches/hmcis-monthly-commentary-may-2016 [Accessed 1 February 2018].

Wyse, D and Torrance, H (2009) The development and consequences of national curriculum assessment for primary education in England. *Educational Research, 51*(2): 213–28.

Zimmerman, B and Dibenedetto, M (2008) Mastery learning and assessment: Implications for students and teachers in an era of high-stakes testing. *Psychology in the School, 45*(3): 206–16.

4
LINKING PLANNING AND ASSESSMENT TOGETHER TO EVIDENCE MASTERY

CHAPTER OBJECTIVES

This chapter will allow you to achieve the following outcomes:

- know how to use the National Curriculum to plan clear learning outcomes;
- know how to map the skills of working scientifically over a unit of work;
- know how to plan for 'cold tasks' that can be used at the beginning of a unit of work.

LINKS TO THE TEACHERS' STANDARDS

S3 – demonstrate good subject and curriculum knowledge

S2 – promote good progress and outcomes by pupils

S4 – plan and teach well-structured lessons

S6 – make accurate and productive use of assessment

```
┌─────────────── LINKS TO THE NATIONAL CURRICULUM ───────────────┐
```

The National Curriculum for science aims to ensure that all pupils: develop scientific knowledge and conceptual understanding through the specific disciplines of biology, chemistry and physics; develop understanding of the nature, processes and methods of science through different types of science enquiries that help them to answer scientific questions about the world around them.

The programmes of study describe a sequence of knowledge and concepts. While it is important that pupils make progress, it is also vitally important that they develop secure understanding of each key block of knowledge and concepts in order to progress to the next stage.

(DfE, 2014)

INTRODUCTION

This chapter will begin by considering the key components of effective science planning. It begins by discussing how to use the National Curriculum to write focused learning objectives and success criteria so that children develop their conceptual understanding and the skill of working scientifically. To ensure that children are progressing, and have the opportunity to apply skills, teachers could 'map' the skills that children will be taught over a unit of work. Therefore, we have modelled how you might achieve this in a grid. It is important that you know children's level of understanding of concepts prior to teaching the unit of work, so the chapter will end by focusing on the use of cold tasks that can be used to assess learning at the beginning of the unit of work.

KEY PRINCIPLES TO CONSIDER WHEN PLANNING A SCIENCE LESSON

Effective planning supports progress in skills and concepts. The starting point for planning is the National Curriculum and identifying what you want the children to learn. The learning objectives are written from attainment targets listed in the National Curriculum. For science, you may have a learning objective for knowledge and another for a skill linked to working scientifically. Once you have written the learning objectives, you then need to think about what the success criteria will be (how will you know if children have been successful in their learning?). Although you will have identified what 'success' will look like, it is useful to ask children to say how they think they can be successful. For example, if you want them to be able to 'gather and record their findings' ask them what success in this might look like. Remind them of the different ways in which they can record, and allow them to decide which is the most appropriate for their work. There is merit in mapping skills that you would like children to develop over the unit of work so that you can plan to teach skills and allow children to apply this to their science work. Table 4.1 provides an example of how skills may be applied to a Year 3 unit of work on plants.

Table 4.1   *Planning for subject knowledge and skills across a unit of work*

Unit of work (Year 3)	Learning objective (subject knowledge)	Learning objective (working scientifically)
Plants	I can identify and describe the functions of different flowering plants (roots, stem/trunk, leaves and flowers).	I can make careful observations of flower parts (e.g. from weeds collected in the school grounds). I can present my observations using labelled diagrams. I can use relevant scientific vocabulary to describe the parts of a plant. I can identify differences and similarities between different plants (trees, grasses and flowering plants).
	I can explore what a plant needs to live and grow (air, light, water, nutrients and room to grow).	I can ask my own questions about plant growth and healthy growth. I can set up my own investigation to explore the variables needed for healthy growth (comparative and fair testing). I can use different equipment to measure accurately. I can record findings using tables and graphs. I can explain what I have found out using scientific vocabulary I can suggest improvements and make further suggestions. I can draw simple conclusions based on the evidence collected.
	I can investigate the way in which water is transported (moved) within plants.	I can ask my own questions about transport of water. I can set up my own test. I can select my own equipment. I can predict what will happen. I can present my findings using pictures/photographs.
	I know the part flowers play in the life cycle.	I can ask my own questions about the life cycles of flowering plants. I can make careful observations of flower parts. I can use relevant language to describe the parts of a plant (I can match words to functions). I can identify differences and similarities between different flowering plants. I can recognise that secondary sources will help me to find out answers to my questions.
	I can give different methods of pollination and seed dispersal.	I can ask simple questions about how plants disperse their seeds and pollen. I can recognise that secondary sources will help me to find out answers to my questions. I can plan my own spinner investigation to explore how seeds are dispersed.

Pupils make progress by building their conceptual understanding over time. Therefore, planning should identify what needs to be taught over a sequence of lessons, rather than in one-hour chunks of time (DfE, 2016). You also need to comprehend that the lesson you have planned is dependent on the interactions with children (these can be unpredictable and requires flexibility in your approach, rather than being a scripted performance, according to John (2006)). There is merit in planning science into blocks of work or thinking about how maths and English lessons can contribute to the science curriculum. Indeed, St Peter's Primary School, North Somerset participated in the Excellence Project, and instead of teaching five or more different subjects during the week in afternoons, they 'block teach' subjects over a week or fortnight (DfE, 2017). As a result of this approach they found the following:

- they were able to teach in depth, ensuring formative assessment in every lesson was strong;

- there were better opportunities for pupils to produce work of greater quality as there was more time for children to work 'at depth' during the week;

- more continuity in learning for pupils – the opportunity to become 'experts' of the week.

However, before delivering a unit of work, you need to find out what children already know, if they have any misconceptions and what they would like to learn in order to make the learning meaningful. We propose that 'cold tasks' can be used to good effect to achieve this aim.

COLD TASKS

The use of 'cold tasks' can provide a wealth of assessment data and can guide your planning and the subsequent learning. The cold tasks can often be revisited at the end of the unit of work to ascertain how the children have progressed in their conceptual understanding. A number of different cold tasks are presented.

KWHL GRIDS

KWHL grids can be used at the beginning of a topic of work so that you can identify what children already know and gaps in understanding, along with any possible naive ideas that they may have. The evidence of prior or current knowledge is added to the first column, where they are asked what they **k**now about a topic. In the second column, children are asked **w**hat they want to find out (and **h**ow they will find out, in the third column). At the end of the unit of work, come back to the KWHL grid and ask the children to consider what they have **l**earnt.

The illustrations in Figure 4.1 show variations to the KWHL girds. In Key Stage 1, the teacher might just plan to have two thought bubbles. It may also be appropriate for the class to only have three columns (what I **k**now, **w**hat I want to find out and what I have **l**earnt).

What I already know.

What I want to find out.

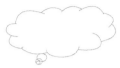

I know ...	I want to find out ...	I have learnt ...

I know ...	I want to find out ...	How I will find it out ...	I have learnt ...

Figure 4.1   Examples of KWHL grids

CONCEPT MAPPING/THOUGHT SHOWERS/MIND MAPPING

Concept mapping, thought showers and mind mapping can all be used at the beginning of a topic and can be revisited at the end in order to show new understanding. A mind map can be thought of as being a little bit like a tree (see Figure 4.2). The concept map may start with the title in the middle of the page and then there are key ideas (the main branches) and the twigs showing further links. It is a good idea to have different colours for the branches and the use of pictures is also encouraged. See the work of Tony Buscan on YouTube for further instructions of how mind mapping may be used.

A concept map shows the links between concepts (see Figure 4.3). For example, if the words 'day' and 'week' appeared on the concept map, the child might add the word 'seven' to show the link (there are seven days in a week). It is a good idea to give children the words so that they are not faced with a blank piece of paper. If children do not know a word, they can circle it – this will provide you with some useful assessment data. The teacher may also consider asking children to complete the concept map in blue at the beginning of the unit of work and green at the end – this will provide evidence of their thinking and how they have connected ideas together. To teach children about concept mapping, teachers may decide to use pictures from films or programmes that children are currently interested in so that they can understand the need to connect ideas together. In Figure 4.3 Harry Potter was used to model how a concept map works. It is best not to provide too many pictures in the first instance, as this may be too overwhelming.

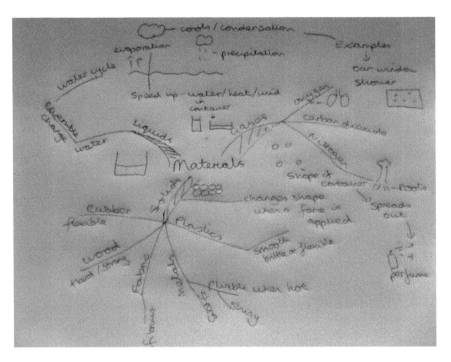

Figure 4.2   Example of a mind map

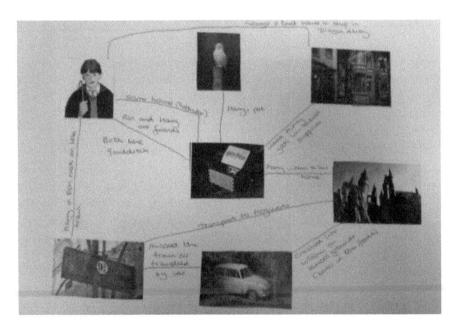

Figure 4.3   Example of concept mapping

(Pictures from the posters were sourced from Pixabay: https://pixabay.com/)

Thought showers (Figure 4.4) are a way of gathering information about a child's understanding. These work well if children are able to work in pairs or small groups so that they have the opportunity to talk about concepts (have your sticky notes ready to jot down any interesting ideas that the children talk about). If you wish to know which children contributed the various ideas, you could ask each child to use a different coloured pencil and add a simple key (or, if one child is scribing, they add the contributing child's initials).

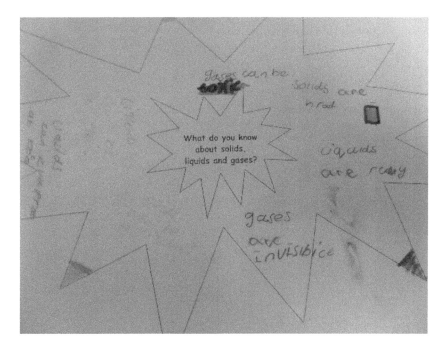

Figure 4.4   Example of a thought shower

WORD SORT

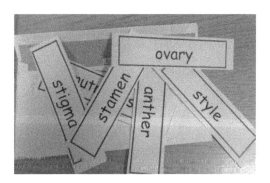

Figure 4.5   Word sort example linked to the topic of plants

Children are given words relating to the topic (the wow words) and are asked to define each word. The words that children are unfamiliar with go into the envelope. These are the words that you know you will need to teach over the duration of the topic. This activity works very well for topics where there is a lot of technical vocabulary.

Figure 4.6 shows an alternative to the word sort. To support children's understanding of scientific words, they could be given some 'wow words' and challenged to think of a question to link the words to an answer. For example, the child may think about the word 'evaporating' and come up with the question: 'Water changing from a liquid to a gas is . . . ?' To take this activity further, children could work in pairs and ask and answer each other questions.

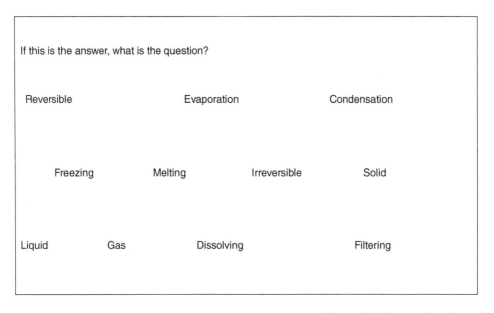

Figure 4.6   Wow words and questions

LABELLING

Children have fun assigning labels to pictures, diagrams (or even themselves, as seen in Figure 4.7). As with the other tasks, you could take a photograph of the labels that children assign at the beginning of the topic and again at the end to show evidence of learning. The activity is active and will help children to remember concepts more readily.

LOOP CARDS

These are used to help children to show their understanding of relationships between concepts. On one side of the card is a statement. The statement links to the answer that is found on another card. You can quickly scan the class to see if they have made a loop (see Figure 4.8 for a completed loop for a plant activity).

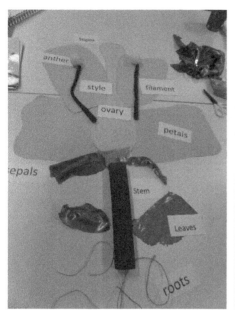

Figure 4.7   Examples of labelling tasks

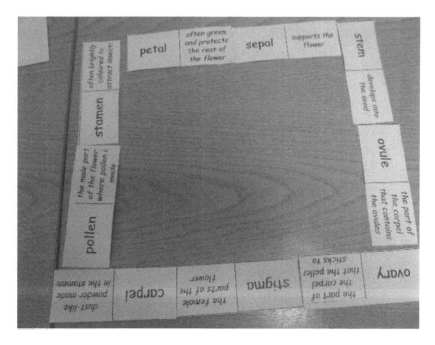

Figure 4.8   Completed loop card task

TRUE/FALSE STATEMENT CARDS

Children sort cards according to whether they are true or false. You could add other categories to the sort such as 'Not Sure' or 'It Depends'. This task works well for subject knowledge but could also be used to develop the skills of working scientifically. For example, would a fair test be the best method of collecting data needed to find out if a magnet is attracted to a material? (Classifying and sorting would be the best approach so the statement should go in the 'false' pile.)

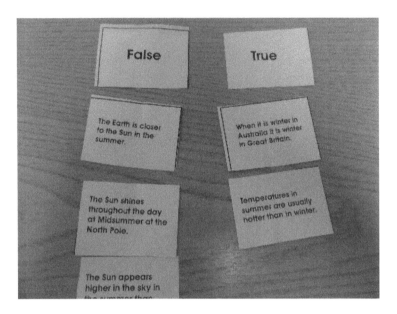

Figure 4.9   Card sorting task

CLASSIFYING AND SORTING

Children could be given a matchbox (see Figure 4.10) and asked to collect materials from around the classroom. From this they can then sort the objects however they wish. The talk generated by this task provides useful assessment data. The task could be undertaken with leaves, plants and plastic animals or toys. An alternative to using a match box could be the use of an egg box.

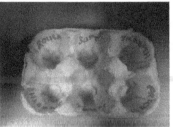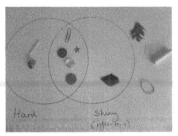

Figure 4.10   Sorting activity using match boxes and egg boxes

CONCEPT CARTOONS

Devised by Naylor and Naylor (2010) concept cartoons encourage children to talk about a concept. Ideally, they should stimulate cognitive conflict and the need to undertake an investigation to check their understanding. Concept cartoons are an effective tool to use at the beginning of a lesson (and at the end to see if children have altered their thinking).

HOT-SEATING

The teacher is in role and children ask questions. This works really well if the teacher is in role as a scientist, as children are able to ask questions about the process of working scientifically. Please be mindful to think about the scientists that you are choosing to use – ensure that you are not reinforcing stereotypes about scientists (e.g. wild hair, glasses and a lab coat!).

ODD ONE OUT

The 'odd-one-out' activity enables you to plan for a discussion point in the lesson. Children look at three pictures, such as those shown in Figure 4.11, talk to each other and decide which the odd one out is. To engage with the task children need to be able to reason and justify their thinking. It is important to stress that there is no correct answer!

Figure 4.11   Pictures that can be used in an odd-one-out cold task

(Remember, there are very good examples that can be found on the Explorify Website.)

An alternative to 'odd one out' could be a positives, minuses and interesting points task. Children are given a statement such as 'What if cats could fly' or 'What if there was no friction' or 'Life without a skeleton'. Children then think of the positives, the minuses and interesting points.

DRAWINGS

Children's drawings can tell us a lot about their thinking and are a useful tool for children who may find it challenging to write (as well as providing a record of children's current level of understanding). Children often have mental models of how things work or look, based upon previous experiences and observations. The drawings can serve as a useful tool to 'probe' children's thinking.

Be aware that some concepts can be a challenge for children to draw. Indeed, Harlen and Qualter (2006) assert that concepts such as evaporation and melting can be hard for children to represent pictorially unless they are provided with key questions such as 'What do you think makes the water level change?'

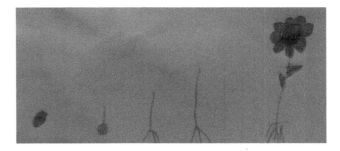

Figure 4.12   Child's drawing showing the growth of a bean

LEARNING TASK

What do you know about a child's thinking based upon this picture? What would be the points for development?

CHAPTER SUMMARY

This chapter has explored how to use the National Curriculum to plan focused learning objectives and success criteria, so that children are able to make progress in their knowledge base, and when working scientifically. We have considered the value of mapping skills over the duration of a unit of work so that children have the opportunity to work as scientists. The chapter concluded by presenting a number of 'cold tasks' that can be used to collect useful assessment data regarding children's understanding of concepts.

USEFUL LINKS

Explorify at: https://explorify.wellcome.ac.uk/

Primary science teaching Trust (Spring News Letter) at:

https://pstt.org.uk/application/files/4915/5196/7104/Spring_2019_Trust_Newsletter.pdf (see pages 20-1 for useful drama links).

REFERENCES

DfE (2014) *The National Curriculum in England: Framework Document*. London: DfE. Available at: https://assets.publishing.service.gov.uk/government/uploads/system/uploads/attachment_data/file/381344/Master_final_national_curriculum_28_Nov.pdf [Accessed 3 January 2019].

DfE (2016) Eliminating unnecessary workload around planning and teaching resources. *Report of the Independent Teacher Workload Review Group*. Available at: www.gov.uk/government/uploads/system/uploads/attachment_data/file/511257/Eliminating-unnecessary-workload-around-planning-and-teaching-resources.pdf

DfE (2017) Doing fewer things in greater depth: How we reduced teacher workload by restructuring our approach to planning. Available at: https://teaching.blog.gov.uk/2017/10/19/doing-fewer-things-in-greater-depth-how-we-reduced-teacher-workload-by-restructuring-our-approach-to-planning/

Harlen, W and Qualter, A (2006) *The Teaching of Science in Primary Schools* (fourth edition). London: David Fulton.

John, D (2006) Lesson planning and the student teacher: Re-thinking the dominant model. *Journal of Curriculum Studies*, *38*(4): 484–98.

Naylor, B and Naylor, S (2010) *Concept Cartoons in Science Education*. Richmond: Millgate House.

Part 2

ASSESSING MASTERY AT 'GREATER DEPTH'

This section is designed for you to 'dip' into in order to support you in your assessment of children's mastery at greater depth in science through practical examples. Each example focuses on one of the attainment targets for the unit of work and provides ideas that can be adapted to other units of work and year groups. It is a good idea to find out what the children know prior to beginning a unit of work by using one of the cold tasks discussed above. The cold tasks may help the teacher to uncover any misconceptions that will need to be challenged. We have provided some of the common misconceptions in relation to each topic area so that you are aware of these. We have also provided a list of typical activities that may be used within a unit of work (please be aware that you would probably not have enough time to cover all of these ideas and it is better to ensure that children have had time to really work as a scientist and to develop their understanding in more depth, rather than having a superficial comprehension of concepts). In each section is a list of key words, and we feel that it would be useful to have these displayed in the classroom because to communicate effectively in science, children need to use scientific vocabulary accurately. Part 2 begins by thinking about good practice in science teaching (and learning) as well as some of the science concepts that children in an Early Years setting may have been exposed to. This understanding will serve to support you in making links to prior learning in Key Stages 1 and 2.

5
SCIENCE IN EARLY YEARS SETTINGS

This chapter will begin by considering the value of helping children to develop a positive attitude towards science and how Personal, Social, Emotional Development (PSED) may be fostered. There will then be a consideration of the importance of purposeful play and engagement when children are developing their 'Understanding the World' (one of the specific areas of learning in the Early Years Foundation Stage Framework where science is closely aligned). The section will conclude by discussing the place of enabling environments and the importance of a skilful adult in ensuring that children make progress through assessment.

DEVELOPING POSITIVE ATTITUDES

Science in the Early Years setting provides many opportunities to develop positive attitudes towards science and it can be argued that learning in the Early Years setting provides the building blocks for later learning. Young children are intuitive scientists and will often notice similarities, differences, patterns and changes. An Early Years setting where curiosity is stimulated and there are opportunities for play and talk can foster positive attitudes towards science. In addition to developing positive attitudes, science can also develop language skills, which has been identified as a predictor of future attainment (DfE, 2017) as the teacher may provide children with key scientific vocabulary. In addition, science is a vehicle to support the following PSED skills due to the collaborative nature of the subject:

- co-operation;
- curiosity;
- reflection;
- independence,

- creativity;

- open-mindedness;

- leadership;

- preservice;

- problem-solving;

- self-esteem;

- sensitivity to living things in the environment;

- self-regulation.

The 'best' learning happens in the Early Years setting when children are engaged in an activity through exploratory play. Indeed, Ephgrave (2018) asserts that when children are engaged in their learning their brain is making connections and learning is taking place. She continues to argue that children are engaged when they have choice over the activities that they wish to explore but this requires time. Children need to have time to acquire skills and knowledge, test ideas, repeat observations in order to make generalisations. Therefore, unless children are engaged in focused teaching activities (often phonics, early mathematics or story time) they should have time to play and explore the indoor and outdoor learning zones that are of interest to them.

To fully engage children with the learning environment in an Early Years setting teachers need to carefully consider how they plan to use the indoor and outdoor learning environments. Early Years settings are often 'zoned' into various areas. If the area is not being used by children, then it needs to be altered as this is not engaging children and is not enabling them to learn. In almost every zone in an Early Years setting, there is the opportunity to develop children's understanding of the world. Table 5.1 shows how various science concepts may be introduced in the Early Years setting through different zones.

Table 5.1 An enabling environment for science learning

Area	Science concepts that can be developed
Sand and water play	Observe items that float and sink. Filtering objects using sieves and funnels. Include sponges to begin the teaching of solids, liquids and gases (observe the bubbles/gases when we squeeze the sponge under the water). Add animals that live in the water (in the winter, ice may form so animals need to be rescued from the ice - introduces thermal insulators).
Role play	Can introduce different occupations that link to science, e.g. a healthcare setting, a vet, a flower shop etc.
Playdough	Children make their own playdough so learn about materials and irreversible changes. Observe forces by pushing, pulling, squeezing and twisting the playdough. Language development linked to material science - flexible, soft, smooth etc.

Music	Have a range of instruments (could be pots and pans or flower pots). Observe the pitch and amplitude of the sound. Feel the vibrations.
Cookery	Observe the processes of mixing, dissolving and melting. Begin to learn about irreversible changes through cooking. Can learn about healthy eating.
Large construction	Learn about pushes and pulls, levers and pullies. Can develop language linked to materials and consider if materials are suited to a function.
Growing area	Can compare leaves, seeds and flowers. Observe life cycles and seasonal changes. Watch food chains in action (can see what feeds on certain plants). May begin to name some mini-beasts, plants and birds.
Climbing/slides	Forces and friction can be observed when climbing or going down slides.
Wheeled toys	Observe the impact of fractional forces by going onto different surfaces.
Dens	Explore material science - consider the 'best' material to build a den. Can explore light and dark (use torches when in the dens).
Pets	If there is a pet, children can learn about the needs of animals and what they need in order to survive.

To develop language skills, consider having books nearby so that research can take place at the point of learning. For example, if a child sees a mini-beast but is unsure of what it is, then books may help them to identify it.

ROLE OF THE ADULT

Every time an adult observes a child, they are listening to what is being said and assessing them before planning and responding to the child. It is good practice to watch the child, wait to be invited into the learning, listen to what is being said and assess and plan the next steps in learning. Ofsted (2017) observed that in good or outstanding settings the following was reported:

> *Many teachers commented that assessment, undertaken as they were teaching, allowed them to adjust their activity in the moment. They believed that this promoted better progress, since the level of challenge or support could be altered quickly to meet children's needs at the time.*

(p26)

It would appear that these teachers were thinking about what they could add to the activity and were looking for a 'teachable moment' when observing children (Ephgrave, 2018). It can, however, be a challenge to know when to interject with a question or an observation because you could be interfering in the learning rather than interacting and challenging the children's thinking. A key message is to 'go with the flow' rather than trying to direct children. Ephgrave (2018) advocates waiting for the child to talk to you and when they do, it is important not to ask too many questions. There is value in modelling language and to provide challenge using phrases such as 'I wonder why …?', showing and suggesting ideas that they could try out.

The Early Years Foundation Stage Profile is the statutory assessment document that needs to be completed at the end of the foundation stage. Many teachers find this process time-consuming and argue that taking photographs and adding notes impacts upon valuable teaching time. It is therefore important to make this manageable for your setting.

CHAPTER SUMMARY

This section considered how the Early Years setting is the starting point for developing positive attitudes towards science. The 'best' learning occurs when children are actively engaged in the learning process, so the environment needs to be carefully planned. Therefore, we have presented a table to exemplify how you might use the zones in an Early Years setting to support the teaching and learning of science. The section concluded by thinking about the role of the adult and how you might most effectively support the learning process.

REFERENCES

DfE (2017) Unlocking talent, fulfilling potential: A plan for improving social mobility through education. London: DfE.

Ephgrave, A (2018) *Planning in the Moment with Young Children: A Practical Guide for Early Years Practitioners and Parents*. London: David Fulton.

Oftsed (2017) Bold beginnings: The Reception curriculum in a sample of good and outstanding schools. London: Ofsted.

6

ACTIVITIES LINKED TO THE NATIONAL CURRICULUM: YEAR 1

PLANTS

ATTAINMENT TARGETS FROM THE NATIONAL CURRICULUM'S PROGRAMME OF STUDY

- identify and name a variety of common wild and garden plants, including deciduous and evergreen trees
- identify and describe the basic structure of a variety of common flowering plants, including trees.

(DfE, 2014, p172)

TYPICAL ACTIVITIES USUALLY ASSOCIATED WITH OR USED IN LESSONS

- Undertaken a welly-walk several times over the year in order to name plants (include trees and grasses) that are found in the local area using simple identification charts or QR Trails. Will focus upon which trees lost their leaves, the shape of leaves and colour of flower/blossoms.

- Taken photographs to help them to talk about how plants change over the seasons.

- Know which flowers might be seen in which season (e.g. tulips, crocuses and daffodils in spring).

- Sorted and grouped plants, seeds and leaves by looking at similarities and differences.

- Undertaken close observations and drawings or rubbings of leaves, seeds and flowers grown in the local area.

- Undertaken labelling activities of pulled up weeds in order to name the basic structure of a plant.

- Related plants to food items, e.g. roots – potatoes and carrots; stems – celery; leaves – cabbages, lettuce; flowers – broccoli, cauliflowers; fruits; nuts.

'WOW WORDS'

Deciduous, evergreen, trees, leaves, stem, flowers (blossom), petals, fruit, roots, seed, truck, branches.

POSSIBLE NAIVE IDEAS THAT MAY NEED TO BE CHALLENGED

- Plants are just found in pots.

- All plants have coloured petals.

- Trees and grasses are not types of plant.

A POSSIBLE RICH TASK TO EVIDENCE 'SECURE MASTERY' OF CONCEPTS

Percy the Park Keeper has been asked to make a list of the trees in the park, but it is wintertime and the deciduous trees have lost their leaves. He is not sure that it is possible to identify the deciduous trees and will have to wait until the summer. Can you help him? The letter below could be used to present the task (ideally children will be familiar with the story of Percy the Park Keeper).

Dear Year 1,

I wonder if you can help me. I have been asked to list the trees that grow in Hotham Park. As you know it is winter and there are not any leaves on the deciduous trees! I have been told that the following trees grow in the park:

- Oak
- Horse chestnut
- Silver birch

- Sycamore
- Beech
- Hazel
- Ash

You will need to act as a bit of a detective to look for clues. I hope to hear from you soon.

Percy

APPLICATION – USE SKILLS FROM BLOOM'S TAXONOMY – SKILL BEYOND RECALL

This task requires the children to first evaluate what they know about identifying plants. It requires them to consider how scientists identify things, e.g. using more than one piece of evidence. They will need to create an identification tool that considers how to identify these trees when there are no leaves, e.g. bark patination.

LOOKING FOR MASTERY AT GREATER DEPTH

- The way they use scientific language (use of words such as leaves, seeds, bark, trunk, twigs, deciduous, evergreen).

- They describe seeds, bark patination and leaf and twig shape and use simple charts to identify the tree types.

- The way they observe the environment to collect evidence (e.g. looking for seeds and leaves that have been dropped by trees and thinking about whether these provide clues about the type of tree nearby).

- The way they compare the features of a range of common trees (e.g. the overall shape of trees).

ANIMALS INCLUDING HUMANS

ATTAINMENT TARGETS FROM THE NATIONAL CURRICULUM'S PROGRAMME OF STUDY

- identify and name a variety of common animals including fish, amphibians, reptiles, birds and mammals

(Continued)

(Continued)

- identify and name a variety of common animals that are carnivores, herbivores and omnivores
- describe and compare the structure of a variety of common animals (fish, amphibians, reptiles, birds and mammals, including pets)
- identify, name, draw and label the basic parts of the human body and say which part of the body is associated with each sense.

(DfE, 2014, pp172-3)

TYPICAL ACTIVITIES USUALLY ASSOCIATED WITH OR USED IN LESSONS

- Sorted and grouped animals according to similarities and differences.
- Used charts and/or internet sources to identify unknown animals.
- Described the basic features of animals of each of the vertebrate groups.
- Used secondary sources to find out about what different animals eat (trip or e-mail correspondence with a zoo keeper; talking to pet owners; trip to pet shop or farm).
- Drawn and named key features of different animals.
- Made own imaginary creature (with labelled features).
- Sang action songs, rhymes and poems linked to body parts, e.g. Simon Says in PE.
- Drawn around partner and labelled body parts using a selection of labels.
- Used feely bags, smelly pots, gone on a sensory walk to know which part of the body is associated with each sense.
- Explored using senses (e.g. my fingers are better at feeling than my elbow).
- Blindfolded sensory activity – guess the object (e.g. hairbrush).
- Explored different materials using their feet – how is this different to using fingers?
- Looked for patterns between people – can taller people jump further, do taller people have bigger feet?
- Used non-standard unit of measure to make comparisons.

'WOW WORDS'

Fish, amphibian, reptile, bird, mammal, beak, ourselves, head, neck, arms, elbows, face, ears, eyes, hair, mouth, teeth, stomach, feet, foot, nose, fingers, skin, knees, textures, sound, smell, touch, see, tall, taller, tallest, similar to, different, difference.

Pair 1 – dog and mouse (both mammals)

Pair 2 – newt and frog (both amphibians)

Pair 3 – blackbird and goldfish (bird and fish)

Figure 6.1

(Pictures sourced from Pixabay: https://pixabay.com/)

POSSIBLE NAIVE IDEAS THAT MAY NEED TO BE CHALLENGED

• May have a limited understanding of the different types of animals – often confusion between reptiles and amphibians.

A POSSIBLE RICH TASK TO EVIDENCE 'SECURE MASTERY' OF CONCEPTS

Gerry wants to be a zoo keeper but tends to get into a bit of a muddle when trying to name different types of animals. Can you name the animals in the pairs in Figure 6.1? Using your skills of observation, can you list as many differences and similarities between the pairs of animals? Do you know which animals are mammals, birds, reptiles, fish or amphibians? Can you think of other examples that would fit into each animal group (e.g. dolphin or whale)? Think of a way of sharing your ideas with Gerry.

APPLICATION – USE SKILLS FROM BLOOM'S TAXONOMY – SKILL BEYOND RECALL

This task will require children to demonstrate that they can name some common animals. It also requires them to consider key features of animal groups (mammals and birds as warm-blooded covered with fur and feathers, and fish, reptiles and amphibians as cold-blooded; fish having scales, reptiles and amphibians having either rough or smooth skin).

LOOKING FOR MASTERY AT GREATER DEPTH

- The way they use scientific language (mammals, reptiles, birds, amphibians, birds, scales, warm or cold blooded, fur, skin).

- Use of observation to classify animals into different groups and will justify reasoning, e.g. This is a mammal because …

- Will be able to give other examples of animals fitting into animal groups – will know that some mammals or reptiles live in water etc.

EVERYDAY MATERIALS

ATTAINMENT TARGETS FROM THE NATIONAL CURRICULUM'S PROGRAMME OF STUDY

- distinguish between an object and the material from which it is made
- identify and name a variety of everyday materials, including wood, plastic, glass, metal, water, and rock
- describe the simple physical properties of a variety of everyday materials
- compare and group together a variety of everyday materials on the basis of their simple physical properties

(DfE, 2014, p173)

Figure 6.2

TYPICAL ACTIVITIES USUALLY ASSOCIATED WITH OR USED IN LESSONS

- Named materials found around the classroom and school.

- Sorted materials and justified why they have been sorted in a certain way.

- Given a range of spoons or cups and identified that they are made from different materials but do the same job – talk about what objects are made from and why, e.g. a range of different types of hats (see Figure 6.2).

- Consumer testing – which is the 'best' material for an umbrella, mopping up a puddle, pet's bedding etc.

'WOW WORDS'

Hard, soft, stretchy, stiff, shiny, dull, rough, smooth, bendy, not bendy, waterproof, absorbent, opaque, transparent, wood, paper, plastic, glass, fabric, elastic, paper, foil, man-made, natural,

POSSIBLE NAIVE IDEAS THAT MAY NEED TO BE CHALLENGED

- Most naive ideas are linked to language, so it is useful to develop children's language skills. Be aware that some children may associate materials with the word fabric. It is useful to use the word materials when talking about solids, liquids and gases.

- Waterproof means it will 'soak up water'.

A POSSIBLE RICH TASK TO EVIDENCE 'SECURE MASTERY' OF CONCEPTS

Building on from one of the typical activities – select an item which the children have not previously looked at. Kitchen utensils are often great for this activity, e.g. metal spatula or spoon. Ask the children to identify the material it is made from. Would it be possible to make it from a different material? If so, what properties does the new material share with the old material? Does it have any properties that the original material does not have? How would these be useful/not useful?

Item	What material is it made from?	Could it be made from another material?	How are the properties of the new material the same?	Are there any different properties to the new material?
Metal spoon				
Paper plate				
Plastic cup				
Hat				

APPLICATION – USE SKILLS FROM BLOOM'S TAXONOMY – SKILL BEYOND RECALL

This activity firstly requires the children to apply what they have learnt about materials to identify the properties. Next, they need to evaluate whether there are any other materials which have similar properties or maybe other properties which would be useful.

LOOKING FOR EVIDENCE OF MASTERY AT GREATER DEPTH

- The way they use scientific language to describe the properties of materials (use of words such as flexible, absorbent, stiff, metal, wood, plastic etc.).

- The way they compare and contrast the properties of materials.

- Will be able to describe and talk about the suitability of materials for a purpose and relate the type of materials to real-life uses.

SEASONAL CHANGE

ATTAINMENT TARGETS FROM THE NATIONAL CURRICULUM'S PROGRAMME OF STUDY

- observe changes across the four seasons
- observe and describe weather associated with the seasons and how day length varies.

(DfE, 2014, p174)

TYPICAL ACTIVITIES USUALLY ASSOCIATED WITH OR USED IN LESSONS

- Will have observed how the weather, plants and clothing they wear changes over the seasons.

- Recorded weather over the week and used appropriate symbols to record findings.

- Made a weather forecast video.

- Created seasonal art, written seasonal poems.

- Adopted a tree in the school grounds (or nearby park) and observed changes over the year.

- Taken a teddy on welly walks over the course of a year and considered what it needs to wear.

- Used colour palettes to observe how colours change in the environment over the year.

- Observed how the day length changes (may have come into school – how is the school different at night?).

'WOW WORDS'

Seasons, summer, spring, autumn, winter, day, night, light, dark, weather, sunny, rain, fog, snow, sleet, hail.

POSSIBLE NAIVE IDEAS THAT MAY NEED TO BE CHALLENGED

- Unaware of changes that take place in the world around them, so first-hand experiences of working outside will challenge thinking.

A POSSIBLE RICH TASK TO EVIDENCE 'SECURE MASTERY' OF CONCEPTS

Present the children with four simple graphs which show the hours of daylight over a period of a year (spring, summer, autumn and winter). These could be factually accurate, or there could be mistakes in them. Then using the concept cartoon idea whereby there are blank speech bubbles for children to add their own ideas, get children to say which they think is which season and why, e.g. I think this is summer as the days are getting longer or there is more sunshine.

APPLICATION – USE SKILLS FROM BLOOM'S TAXONOMY – SKILL BEYOND RECALL

This activity encourages the children to use their skills of evaluation to firstly consider what their graph is showing them. They then need to consider what they know about the seasons and consider how this might be shown in a simple graph (synthesise). They then need to explain this.

LOOKING FOR EVIDENCE OF MASTERY AT GREATER DEPTH

- The way they use scientific evidence to describe the changes in day length over the year.

- Will be able to name the four seasons and will know the months that they occur.

- Will talk about the different features of seasons and will relate to their lives in terms of changes.

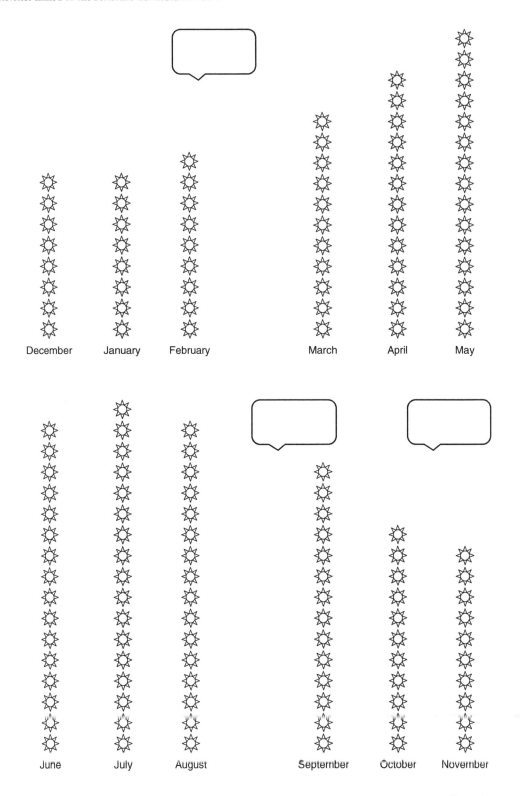

Figure 6.3

7

ACTIVITIES LINKED TO THE NATIONAL CURRICULUM: YEAR 2

LIVING THINGS AND THEIR HABITATS

TYPICAL ACTIVITIES USUALLY ASSOCIATED WITH OR USED IN LESSONS

- Sorted items, found in the local area, into those that are living, dead and never lived.
- Observed, drawn and labelled animals found during a Bug Hunt.
- Used 'spotter sheets' to identify animals and plants in local habitats.

- Described the conditions of different micro-habitats in the school grounds.

- Created simple food chains for a familiar habitat that they have visited (e.g. school grounds, wooded area, pond and/or beach) from first-hand observations and research.

- Created simple food chains from books (e.g. *The Spider and the Fly* by DiTerlizzi, *The Gruffalo* by Donaldson or *Guess Who's Coming to Dinner?* authored by Tinknell and Kelly). You could use books, such as *The Hungry Caterpillar* by Carle, where the food chains are not correct (the page where the caterpillar eats a range of unusual foods is a useful page).

- Sorted and matched animals and plants to different habitats and micro-habitats.

- Compared contrasting habitats and the animals and plants living in different habitats (rainforest compared to polar region).

- Helped to make a Bug Hotel.

- Made own diorama (habitat in a shoe box). This activity is time-consuming so might be a useful homework task so that parents can engage in the learning with their children.

'WOW WORDS'

Habitat, micro-habitat (stones, leaf litter, path), shelter, warmth, ocean, rainforests, desert, polar region, woodland, seashore, living, not-living, alive, food chain, energy, predator, prey, life processes.

Title – where is the holiday?

Drawing of the holiday setting (could include a map showing key features such as an open woodland and a nearby pond)	Things to do:	Nice things to eat!

Figure 7.1

(Picture sourced from Pixabay: https://pixabay.com/)

POSSIBLE NAIVE IDEAS THAT MAY NEED TO BE CHALLENGED

- Fire, clouds and toys are living as they move.

- Seeds are not alive (consider the idea of dormancy).

- Confusion relating to the arrow in the food chain – thinking the arrow means 'eats'; also be aware of incorrect food chains that have been presented in picture and story books.

A POSSIBLE RICH TASK TO EVIDENCE 'SECURE MASTERY' OF CONCEPTS

Mrs Grass Snake is looking for her perfect holiday destination but nothing in the holiday brochures have all the things she needs for the holiday to feel like a home away from home. Can you design a resort which will have everything that she needs? Remember to consider what will be on the menu, what is special about her room, what activities will be available during the stay. Figure 7.1 is an example of a sheet that could be used to scaffold children's thinking.

APPLICATION – USE SKILLS FROM BLOOM'S TAXONOMY – SKILL BEYOND RECALL

This activity requires the child to research an individual animal and apply this knowledge to create a poster/advert which demonstrates that they have a secure understanding of the term 'habitat'.

LOOKING FOR EVIDENCE OF MASTERY AT GREATER DEPTH

- Will be able to describe how the holiday destination (habitat) will be suited to a reptile's needs.

- Will be able to name a variety of plants and animals that the grass snake will come into contact with while on holiday.

- Will be able to describe what the grass snake will eat.

- Will be able to say if a grass snake is suited to live in more than one type of habitat and why.

PLANTS

ATTAINMENT TARGETS FROM THE NATIONAL CURRICULUM'S PROGRAMME OF STUDY

- observe and describe how seeds and bulbs grow into mature plants
- find out and describe how plants need water, light and a suitable temperature to grow and stay healthy.

(DfE, 2014, 176)

TYPICAL ACTIVITIES USUALLY ASSOCIATED WITH OR USED IN LESSONS

- Drawn seeds and bulbs using careful observations.

- Compared similarities and differences between bulbs and seeds.

- Grown a range of bulbs and seeds and compared how they grow (up for beans or runners for strawberries).

- Grown seeds on different materials (cotton wool, cardboard, sand, soil etc.)

- Taken photographs/drawn pictures and matched simple labels to the stages of a plant's growth.

- Looked after plants as they grow (awareness of weeding, watering, thinning – good if growing carrots or sweet peas).

- Made close observations and measurements as plants grow.

- Researched when the best time to grow seeds and bulbs is by looking at packets of seeds (a good book to use here is *The Story of Frog Belly Ratbone* by Ering).

- Written instructions for seed packets.

- Visited an allotment or local garden centre to talk about growing seeds and bulbs and conditions needed for healthy growth.

- Observed which plants grow best in certain places (e.g. where do we find the most daisies on the school field?).

'WOW WORDS'

Seeds, bulbs, water, light, temperature, growth, healthy.

POSSIBLE NAIVE IDEAS THAT MAY NEED TO BE CHALLENGED

- All seeds and bulbs look the same.

- All seeds take the same time to germinate.

- All plants grow in the same way.

A POSSIBLE RICH TASK TO EVIDENCE 'SECURE MASTERY' OF CONCEPTS

Present the children with pictures of plants which are not growing healthily (see Figure 7.2). This could be in the context of Mr Grow who is growing plants for the summer fête but has noticed some problems. Ask the children if they can predict what the issues might be, e.g. a plant with shrivelled leaves may not be getting enough water, or it could be a sign that it is being kept in too hot a condition. Ask the children how they might set up an experiment to prove they are correct. This will also give them the opportunity to demonstrate mastery of 'working scientifically'. You could take children around the school to look for plants that are not growing very well and get them to predict why that might be the case.

Figure 7.2

APPLICATION – USE SKILLS FROM BLOOM'S TAXONOMY – SKILL BEYOND RECALL

This reverse engineering of an experiment can be used with many science concepts. It requires the children to first recall their experiences from lessons and wider experiences to consider. They need to then evaluate whether this is similar to what they are seeing in the pictures in order to solve the problem.

LOOKING FOR EVIDENCE OF MASTERY AT GREATER DEPTH

- Will be able to make comparisons between the different plants (e.g. height, colour, texture of leaves).

- Will be able to describe the conditions needed for plants to grow well (water, light and a suitable temperature).

- Will be able to make close observations of plants and will begin to predict what is wrong with them.

ANIMALS INCLUDING HUMANS

ATTAINMENT TARGETS FROM THE NATIONAL CURRICULUM'S PROGRAMME OF STUDY

- notice that animals, including humans, have offspring which grow into adults
- find out about and describe the basic needs of animals, including humans, for survival (water, food and air)
- describe the importance for humans of exercise, eating the right amounts of different types of food, and hygiene.

(DfE, 2014, p176)

TYPICAL ACTIVITIES USUALLY ASSOCIATED WITH OR USED IN LESSONS

- Matched pictures to off-spring (chicken – chick, calf – cow, tadpole – frog and caterpillar – butterfly).

- Observed animals growing over a period of time (e.g. caterpillars to butterflies, eggs to chicks, frog spawn to frog, babies to adults).

- Used research to create a book on life cycles for children in Year R or Year 1.

- Trip to farm/zoo to see how adults are different and similar to offspring.

- Sorted cards to show essentials for survival.

- Compared photos of them as a baby to now.

- Posed their own questions about basic needs for survival and answered these by asking a parent of a baby.

- Explored how exercise affects their body.

- Classified food in a range of ways using the Eatwell plate.

- Know that different amounts of food are needed at different stages of life.

- Analysed a meal using the Eatwell plate.

- Cooked pizzas and compared which are more balanced.

- Investigated hand-washing using glitter bug gel to show how microbes may be spread.

- Used an aerosol spray to investigate how far a sneeze travels.

'WOW WORDS'

Survival, water, air, food, adult, baby, offspring, kitten, calf, puppy, pupa, spawn, tadpole, frog, exercise, hygiene, baby, toddler, child, teenager, adult, exercise.

POSSIBLE NAIVE IDEAS THAT MAY NEED TO BE CHALLENGED

- Thinking that foods are 'good' or 'bad' rather than understanding the importance of balanced diets or healthy/unhealthy diets.

- Growing only happens when asleep.

- Associating the word 'growth' with stretching or increasing in length, without adding more material.

A POSSIBLE RICH TASK TO EVIDENCE 'SECURE MASTERY' OF CONCEPTS

Present the children with Eatwell plates (one for an omnivore, one for a vegetarian, and one for a vegan, as shown in Figure 7.3). Think about providing a multi-cultural Eatwell plate, if it reflects the

This is not a balanced diet because there is no meat.

There are not enough of the different types of protein.

Figure 7.3

needs of your class. On the outside have a speech bubble(s) that says not all the plates can be a balanced diet for a human as they do not all have meat. Ask the children to explain what they think? See Figure 7.3 for an example for the vegetarian Eatwell plate.

APPLICATION – USE SKILLS FROM BLOOM'S TAXONOMY – SKILL BEYOND RECALL

This task requires the children to have a deep understanding that a balanced diet consists of a balance of nutrients the human body needs to function, e.g. protein to build or repair tissues. The children have to evaluate the plates to identify which items are providing protein in the absence of meat.

LOOKING FOR EVIDENCE OF MASTERY AT GREATER DEPTH

- Will be able to describe the importance of eating the right amounts of different types of food.

- Will be able to name the types of food in each section of the Eatwell plate.

EVERYDAY MATERIALS

ATTAINMENT TARGETS FROM THE NATIONAL CURRICULUM'S PROGRAMME OF STUDY

- identify and compare the suitability of a variety of everyday materials, including wood, metal, plastic, glass, brick, rock, paper and cardboard for particular uses
- find out how the shapes of solid objects made from some materials can be changed by squashing, bending, twisting and stretching.

(DfE, 2014, p177)

TYPICAL ACTIVITIES USUALLY ASSOCIATED WITH OR USED IN LESSONS

- Classified and sorted objects from around the school.

- Made suggestions about the suitability of materials for a task (and will know that some materials are good for a range of purposes).

- Know that some materials are not suitable for a particular purpose, e.g. a chocolate teapot; cardboard for a window; a jumper made from glass.

- Researched people who have found new materials, e.g. Dunlop.

- Tested the properties of materials for use (the film *The Incredibles* would be a relevant and motivating link to make) when encouraging children to invent a new material for a superhero.

- Explored how materials can be changed by bending, stretching, twisting.

- Will have used scientific words correctly to name and describe the properties of materials.

- Applied learning by designing a box for a purpose (use the book *Egg Drop* by Grey to provide a hook for children to make a box using suitable materials to keep the egg safe).

'WOW WORDS'

Reinforce words from Year 1 plus squashing, twisting, bending, stretching.

POSSIBLE NAIVE IDEAS THAT MAY NEED TO BE CHALLENGED

- Knowing the origins of materials (cotton from plants; leather from animals; wool from sheep).

- Language issues – continue to reinforce 'wow words' from Year 1.

A POSSIBLE RICH TASK TO EVIDENCE 'SECURE MASTERY' OF CONCEPTS

Present the children with the following problem: Is it possible to build a 30cm bridge between two tables, which can support a weight of 200g? Today we only have paper (newspaper) and a little tape. It is important to limit the tape that is given, otherwise the structure will just be tape. Once the

Figure 7.4

children have built their bridge, ask them to look at some pictures of different bridges (wooden, steel, concrete). Ask them to explain why paper is not used to make commercial bridges? Help the children to focus on the suitability based on the properties of paper. To add another dimension, the bridges could be exposed to wind and rain so that children are supported to make the link between the properties of a material and their uses. This activity links well to design technology and a STEM approach to learning. Figure 7.4 shows an example of a bridge.

APPLICATION – USE SKILLS FROM BLOOM'S TAXONOMY – SKILL BEYOND RECALL

This activity requires the children to evaluate the properties of paper against other materials in order to explain/justify why it is not used to build bridges outside of the classroom. It also requires them to use their knowledge of the properties of paper in order to create the bridge, e.g. if you roll the paper into a tight tube it improves its strength.

LOOKING FOR EVIDENCE OF MASTERY AT GREATER DEPTH

- Will be able to compare the suitability of materials for a use (bridge-building).

- Will test paper and use findings to say why bridges are not usually made from paper.

- Will be able to say why paper would not be the best material to make a bridge from in real-life contexts.

8

ACTIVITIES LINKED TO THE NATIONAL CURRICULUM: YEAR 3

PLANTS

TYPICAL ACTIVITIES USUALLY ASSOCIATED WITH OR USED IN LESSONS

- Looked for plants in unusual places (gutter, roof, cracks in pavement etc.).

- Annotated plants according to name and function, e.g. leaves are the factories of the plant and make food for the plant, or used a card sort – matching name of plant to function.

- Applied annotated labelling to other plants such as a cactus or Venus flytrap.

- Created a 'new' species of flowering plant.

- Observed what happens to plants if the roots or leaves are removed.

- Observed the impact of putting white carnations into coloured water (transport of water through the plant).

- Observed what happens if the plant is not given enough water (becomes flaccid).

- Observed what happens when conditions are changed (dark cupboards, cold, deprived of air, different soil types, fertilisers, space etc.).

- Observed flowers being visited by pollinators – which colour petal is most popular?

- Observed seed dispersal from first-hand experiences of sycamore, horse chestnuts, sweet chestnuts, acorns, lime seeds, dandelion, burdock and secondary sources for sea beans, coconut, spitting cucumbers etc. (could add own narration to a section of the Life of Plants).

- Explored which is the 'best' spinner while exploring seed dispersal.

- Classified seeds according to how they are dispersed (wind, animal, water).

- Grown beans through the life cycle from seed to seed and used correct vocabulary for each stage (germination, pollination, fertilisation and seed dispersal).

- Linked with a school in another part of the country to find out if plants of the same species (e.g. daffodils) flower at different times.

'WOW WORDS'

Air, light, water, nutrients, soil, reproduction, transportation, dispersal, pollination, flower.

POSSIBLE NAIVE IDEAS THAT MAY NEED TO BE CHALLENGED

- Language linked to germination and growth.

- Soil provides support (rather than providing nutrients).

- Seeds need light to germinate.

A POSSIBLE RICH TASK TO EVIDENCE 'SECURE MASTERY' OF CONCEPTS

Present the children with a piece of celery (remove any leaves and make a fresh cut along the bottom) in a cup of water (mixed with red food dye). On the table have some responses in speech bubbles, e.g. I think the celery will turn red just like the carnation flower (it is important that the children have seen the carnation experiment); I think that it will not turn red as the celery does not have a flower like the carnation. Have a blank speech bubble for the children to put their ideas in if they do not agree with any of the presented comments.

Figure 8.1

(Picture sourced from Pixabay: https://pixabay.com/)

APPLICATION – USE SKILLS FROM BLOOM'S TAXONOMY – SKILL BEYOND RECALL

This activity requires the children to evaluate what a stick of celery is. Children who have a deep understanding of plants will realise that it is a plant stem and, therefore, may have the same structures for transporting water and nutrients around the plant as the carnation. Therefore, the coloured food dye will be transported up through the stem to other structures in the plant. A picture on an interactive whiteboard (e.g. one similar to Figure 8.1) could be used to talk through the parts of the plant.

LOOKING FOR EVIDENCE OF MASTERY AT GREATER DEPTH

- Will be able to describe the function of the stem in a plant using observations to support their explanations.

- Will understand the structures of different plants and how water is transported (may compare the structure of a carnation stem with the celery or a tree trunk).

- Will explain observations made during the investigation.

- Will link the transportation of water through a plant to the transportation of minerals.

ANIMALS INCLUDING HUMANS

ATTAINMENT TARGETS FROM THE NATIONAL CURRICULUM'S PROGRAMME OF STUDY

- identify that animals, including humans, need the right types and amount of nutrition, and that they cannot make their own food; they get nutrition from what they eat
- identify that humans and some other animals have skeletons and muscles for support, protection and movement.

(DfE, 2014, p182)

TYPICAL ACTIVITIES USUALLY ASSOCIATED WITH OR USED IN LESSONS

- Explored why a balanced diet is needed and the impact of having too much or not enough of the various groups.

- Looked at food labels to answer questions – how much sugar and fat – compared different brands and how they label food items.

- Planned daily diets for certain groups of people (if doing the Second World War, *Rational Food* has some good case studies; see reference on page 139). Other effective links can be made to history – comparing diets of the past to the diets of today.

- Presented findings about nutrients in different food items such as pizza.

- Looked at X-ray pictures – where in the body is the bone? Placed the X-ray in the correct part on an outline of the body.

- Labelled key bones in the body (skull, spine, ribcage).

- Considered how animals with exoskeletons might be protected and how they move.

- Used a secondary source to research the function of the skeleton.

- Made models of how the skeleton helps movement.

- Undertaken pattern-seeking investigations – can people with bigger hands pick up more sweets, etc.

'WOW WORDS'

Movement, muscles, bones, skull, skeleton, nutrition, fat, sugar, carbohydrate, protein, vitamins, minerals, dairy produce, meat, fruit, vegetables, diet.

POSSIBLE NAIVE IDEAS THAT MAY NEED TO BE CHALLENGED

- Size and shape of different bones and how they protect organs.

A POSSIBLE RICH TASK TO EVIDENCE 'SECURE MASTERY' OF CONCEPTS

Present the children with the daily diet for an athlete. Ask them to compare it to their own daily diet. How are the two diets similar and different? Why are they similar and different? Alternatively, you could alter the scenario to suit the area of the curriculum that is being studied, e.g. could compare the diet of a person during the Second World War (see Figure 8.2) to today or could look at the evidence for the diet of a Palaeolithic (Stone Age) person and compare to today etc.

Figure 8.2

(Pictures sourced from Pixabay: https://pixabay.com/)

APPLICATION – USE SKILLS FROM BLOOM'S TAXONOMY – SKILL BEYOND RECALL

This task requires the children to evaluate the two diets, e.g. how are they the same and different? Children with a deep understanding will be able to identify that the same food groups exist in both (e.g. balanced diets) and will know that this is because an athlete (Stone Age diet or person from WWII) is still a human. They will also make the link for the increased amount of food and key food groups to allow the athlete increased exercise or in the case of a WWII diet, the impact of rationing. The 'balance' of the Palaeolithic diet will be dependent upon where the person lives – if near a lake or the sea, the diet will contain more protein, from seafood. Children should be made aware that the dairy products will not exist in early Palaeolithic diets due to the hunter-gatherer lifestyle.

LOOKING FOR EVIDENCE OF MASTERY AT GREATER DEPTH

- Will have an understanding that some diets have more of one food group than another and will consider the impact of this in terms of providing a balanced diet.

- Will be able to talk about the nutrient content of different diets and the impact of this on health.

ROCKS

ATTAINMENT TARGETS FROM THE NATIONAL CURRICULUM'S PROGRAMME OF STUDY

- compare and group together different kinds of rocks on the basis of their appearance and simple physical properties
- describe in simple terms how fossils are formed when things that have lived are trapped within rock
- recognise that soils are made from rocks and organic matter.

(DfE, 2014, p182)

TYPICAL ACTIVITIES USUALLY ASSOCIATED WITH OR USED IN LESSONS

- Observed rocks closely in order to classify according to features.

- Sorted rocks according to types.

- Investigated the hardness of rocks.

- Investigated how absorbent rocks are.

- Investigated which rock is best, e.g. a statue in the school grounds.

- Observed how rocks change over time (looked at buildings and gravestones for evidence).

- Researched how fossils are formed and made own flicker books/video or comic strip to explain the process.

- Classified soils and researched how soil is formed (the book *Pebble in my Pocket* is a good hook to the lesson) and presented findings using role play or comic strips.

- Tested how well different soils retain water (links can be made to growing plants in different soil types).

- Observed how soils can be separated (see activities on Practical Action website: **https://practical action.org**).

- Researched the work of palaeontologist Mary Anning.

- If possible, looked for fossils.

'WOW WORDS'

Fossils, soils, sandstone, marble, pumice, crystals, absorbent, clay, sedimentary rock, similarities, differences.

POSSIBLE NAIVE IDEAS THAT MAY NEED TO BE CHALLENGED

- Bricks and concrete are types of rocks.

A POSSIBLE RICH TASK TO EVIDENCE 'SECURE MASTERY' OF CONCEPTS

Give the children a slate roof tile (and some slate pieces) and some other waterproof rocks. Ask the children why slate is used or has been used in the past for roof tiles. Why have humans not used other waterproof rocks? Ask the children to consider why clay tiles are also widely used. How are they similar and/or different to slate tiles? It is better to have the actual rocks but pictures, such as Figure 8.3, can clearly show the properties of slate.

Figure 8.3

(Picture sourced from Pixabay: https://pixabay.com/)

APPLICATION – USE SKILLS FROM BLOOM'S TAXONOMY – SKILL BEYOND RECALL

This activity requires the children to use a deep understanding of the properties of rock. A close examination of the slate will make visible the foliations. It is because of these that when the rock is hit parallel to a foliation the slate splits into flat, lighter sheets of stone. Granite, although waterproof does not share this property, which means it can only be cut by machine. This activity requires the children to evaluate why slate is used for roof tiles instead of other waterproof rock.

LOOKING FOR EVIDENCE OF MASTERY AT GREATER DEPTH

- Will know the physical properties of rocks are suited to a particular purpose.

- Will be able to describe rocks using appropriate scientific vocabulary (metamorphic and foliations impermeable).

- Will draw conclusions about the properties of slate and how it is suited to a purpose.

LIGHT

ATTAINMENT TARGETS FROM THE NATIONAL CURRICULUM'S PROGRAMME OF STUDY

- recognise that they need light in order to see things and that dark is the absence of light
- notice that light is reflected from surfaces
- recognise that light from the sun can be dangerous and that there are ways to protect their eyes
- recognise that shadows are formed when the light from a light source is blocked by a solid object
- find patterns in the way that the size of shadows change.

(DfE, 2014, p183)

TYPICAL ACTIVITIES USUALLY ASSOCIATED WITH OR USED IN LESSONS

- Viewed objects in a dark box. Experienced darkness, e.g. a dark tent.

- Explored how different surfaces reflect or absorb light.

- Explored the impact of changing the brightness of a room.

- Explored how shadows are formed.

- Matched shadows to the object that made the shadow.

- Made a puppet show using transparent, translucent and opaque objects.

- Explored how moving the light source impacts upon shadow size and clarity.

- Used 'finger lights' to mix colours of light (all colours make white).

- To know how to protect skin and eyes from the rays of the sun – design the best sunglasses (the use of UV beads can be a good hook to teach about UV light).

- Light and art workshops – looked at artists and considered how they use light and dark.

'WOW WORDS'

Light, dark, shadows, mirror, shiny, smooth, rough, surfaces, reflective.

POSSIBLE NAIVE IDEAS THAT MAY NEED TO BE CHALLENGED

- The eyes are an active organ (rather than a receptive organ) in the process of seeing.

- Shiny objects are sources of light.

- The moon is a source of light.

A POSSIBLE RICH TASK TO EVIDENCE 'SECURE MASTERY' OF CONCEPTS

Present the children with the following question: Is it possible to have a red shadow? Why? Ask the children to record their discussions. Figure 8.4 shows how you might set up the investigation.

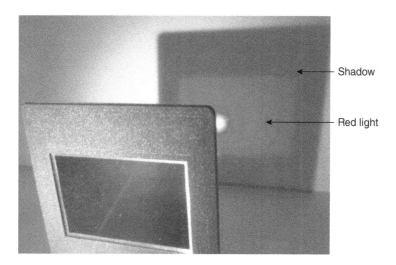

Figure 8.4

An alternative to the above would be to encourage children to think about why a footballer has four shadows when playing on a floodlit pitch or is it possible to have more than one shadow?

APPLICATION – USE SKILLS FROM BLOOM'S TAXONOMY – SKILL BEYOND RECALL

This activity requires the children to have a deep understanding of what a shadow is. They have to evaluate their knowledge against the question in order to come up with an answer.

LOOKING FOR EVIDENCE OF MASTERY AT GREATER DEPTH

- Will know that shadows are formed by blocking light by a solid (opaque) object so are normally black.

- Will know that using a red filter will mean that red light will pass through the filter and shine on the wall (see above).

FORCES AND MAGNETS

ATTAINMENT TARGETS FROM THE NATIONAL CURRICULUM'S PROGRAMME OF STUDY

- compare how things move on different surfaces
- notice that some forces need contact between two objects, but magnetic forces can act at a distance
- observe how magnets attract or repel each other and attract some materials and not others
- compare and group together a variety of everyday materials on the basis of whether they are attracted to a magnet, and identify some magnetic materials
- describe magnets as having two poles
- predict whether two magnets will attract or repel each other, depending on which poles are facing.

(DfE, 2014, p184)

TYPICAL ACTIVITIES USUALLY ASSOCIATED WITH OR USED IN LESSONS

- Identified pushes and pulls from around the school.

- Explored how objects move on different surfaces: cars on ramps, balloon rockets, toys, hover-crafts, zip wires.

- Played and devised games that require low levels of friction (air hockey).

- Considered the benefits and issues of friction – what if there was no friction?
- Explored the work of Dunlop and tyres.
- Explored and grouped which materials are attracted to a magnet.
- Observed how magnets behave and use language correctly (attract, repel).
- Explored the use of magnets in everyday life.
- Explored how materials work at a distance (through a table, in water, moving paperclips).
- Investigated the strength of magnets.

'WOW WORDS'

Magnetic force, force, contact, attract, repel, friction, poles, push, pull.

POSSIBLE NAIVE IDEAS THAT MAY NEED TO BE CHALLENGED

- All metals are magnetic.
- Magnets do not work in water/liquids.

A POSSIBLE RICH TASK TO EVIDENCE 'SECURE MASTERY' OF CONCEPTS

Show the children a picture of a levitating pen (see Figure 8.5). If you have the real item, this would be better. Ask the children to use their knowledge of magnets and forces to explain how this works. Get them to draw a diagram with labels to illustrate the explanation. Can they use this knowledge to make their own levitating pencil? If it does not work, are they able to consider why this might be the case?

Figure 8.5

Hint – this is a useful website should you wish to make your own levitating pencil: **https://youtu.be/RXs3EpSDFF4**.

APPLICATION – USE SKILLS FROM BLOOM'S TAXONOMY – SKILL BEYOND RECALL

This requires the children to recall their knowledge of magnets and synthesise this information to what they are observing in the levitating pen. They can then use this knowledge to create their own version.

LOOKING FOR EVIDENCE OF MASTERY AT GREATER DEPTH

- Will know that magnetic objects can act at a distance (repelling force).

- Can decide on an approach to solve a problem using knowledge of magnets and that like poles attract and unlike poles repel.

9
ACTIVITIES LINKED TO THE NATIONAL CURRICULUM: YEAR 4

LIVING THINGS AND THEIR HABITATS

TYPICAL ACTIVITIES USUALLY ASSOCIATED WITH OR USED IN LESSONS

- Used classification keys to name unknown plants and animals.

- Created own simple identification key to group living things.

Figure 9.1

(Picture sourced from Pixabay: https://pixabay.com/)

- Explored the impact of humans on the local environment.

- Written letters, delivered an assembly – e.g. plastic pollution.

- Engaged with local authority about local areas and made change happen.

- Found out how local areas have changed.

- Observed plants and animals in different habitats.

'WOW WORDS'

Fish, amphibians, reptiles, birds, mammals, herbivore, carnivore, omnivore, invertebrates, slug, snail, worms, spiders, insects, vertebrates, group, classify, environment, habitats.

POSSIBLE NAIVE IDEAS THAT MAY NEED TO BE CHALLENGED

- Difficulties in assigning animals and plants to different groups.

A POSSIBLE RICH TASK TO EVIDENCE 'SECURE MASTERY' OF CONCEPTS

Present the children with the Natural History Museum information sheet on common UK house spiders (**www.nhm.ac.uk/content/dam/nhmwww/take-part/identify-nature/spiders-in-your-home-id-guide.pdf**). Ask the children to create an identification key to help the class identify the spiders in their homes from the information provided. Ask the children to compare their key with others. Are they all the same? Is so, why? If not, why? Do all the keys work, e.g. Iden tify the different species of spider?

APPLICATION – USE SKILLS FROM BLOOM'S TAXONOMY – SKILL BEYOND RECALL

The task requires the children to use their knowledge of keys to create their own identification key. This task is especially challenging as the animals are from the same species, so it is not just as simple as counting the legs. The children will need to consider the scientific language, e.g. abdomen and cephalothorax; season; size; movement; and construction of the web.

LOOKING FOR EVIDENCE OF MASTERY AT GREATER DEPTH

- Will be able to use technical vocabulary in order to construct their own identification key based upon observable features of the spiders.

- Will be required to consider key questions (and answers) that will help to sort and classify each of the spiders.

ANIMALS INCLUDING HUMANS

ATTAINMENT TARGETS FROM THE NATIONAL CURRICULUM'S PROGRAMME OF STUDY

- describe the simple functions of the basic parts of the digestive system in humans
- identify the different types of teeth in humans and their simple functions
- construct and interpret a variety of food chains, identifying producers, predators and prey.

(DfE, 2014, p186)

TYPICAL ACTIVITIES USUALLY ASSOCIATED WITH OR USED IN LESSONS

- Researched the function of the digestive system (augmented reality – Curiscope is a useful resource (**www.curiscope.com/**).

- Sequenced what happens in the digestive system.

- Created a model of the digestive system and a booklet to explain what happens in each part.

- Explored eating food and the functions of different teeth (track the journey of an apple through the mouth).

- Made a dental record of the teeth in their mouth (looked at dental records).

- Used modelling clay or plasticine to make a model of the teeth in their mouth (focusing on shape of different teeth).

- Had a visit from a dental nurse to learn about oral hygiene.

- Explored the impact of different drinks on teeth using egg shells.

- Classified animals into herbivore, omnivores and carnivores according to teeth (good idea to work with local museums/zoos in order for children to look at actual animal skulls).

- Used food chains to identify producers, prey and predators within different habitats and identified the flow of energy.

'WOW WORDS'

Mouth, tongue, teeth, incisors, canines, pre-molars, molars, oesophagus, stomach, small intestine, large intestine, digestive system, food chain, energy.

POSSIBLE NAIVE IDEAS THAT MAY NEED TO BE CHALLENGED

- Issues with language – misunderstanding of predators and prey or the names and functions of the digestive system.

- The digestive system is just a tube.

- Positioning of key organs – often the stomach.

- Teeth do the same job.

A POSSIBLE RICH TASK TO EVIDENCE 'SECURE MASTERY' OF CONCEPTS

Present the children with a variety of animals, plants and fungi found in a woodland environment. Ask the children to create a food chain from the things provided. Coloured wool can be particularly helpful to enable the children to see the links (see Figure 9.2). The children who have a deep understanding of food chains will be able to demonstrate that they are more complex than a single line, with many species feeding on more than one other species. Once the children have completed the food chain, ask them questions regarding what would happen if certain species were removed/exterminated from the food chain? For example, if small insect-eating species were removed, this could result in an insect population explosion until they exhausted their food sources.

APPLICATION – USE SKILLS FROM BLOOM'S TAXONOMY – SKILL BEYOND RECALL

This task requires the children to use their skills of synthesis and evaluation in order to predict the consequences of removing species from a particular food chain. It requires a deep understanding of the terms: producers, predators and prey.

LOOKING FOR EVIDENCE OF MASTERY AT GREATER DEPTH

- Will identify common living things that can be found in a habitat (e.g. woodland).

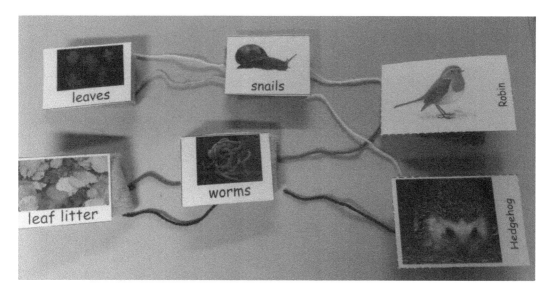

Figure 9.2

- Will use scientific language associated with food chains (producer, predator, prey, primary consumer, composer).

- Will know that a food chain is a flow of energy and will be able to consider what will happen if part of the food chain is missing (e.g. from the above example will pose and answer questions – what would happen if the snails reduced in numbers).

STATES OF MATTER

ATTAINMENT TARGETS FROM THE NATIONAL CURRICULUM'S PROGRAMME OF STUDY

- compare and group materials together, according to whether they are solids, liquids or gases
- observe that some materials change state when they are heated or cooled, and measure or research the temperature at which this happens in degrees Celsius (°C)
- identify the part played by evaporation and condensation in the water cycle and associate the rate of evaporation with temperature.

(DfE, 2014, p106)

Figure 9.3
(Picture sourced from Pixabay: https://pixabay.com/)

TYPICAL ACTIVITIES USUALLY ASSOCIATED WITH OR USED IN LESSONS

- Observed and classified a range of solids, liquids and gases (have some unusual ones such as foams, gels, pastes, jelly, mists, sand etc.).

- Made gases visible, e.g. squeezed sponges under water to see the release of bubbles, opening fizzy water, blowing bubbles into water, observing wind in the trees.

- Observed melting materials – chocolate, butter.

- Observed changes when cooking materials.

- Explored ice balloons or ice hands (rubber gloves filled with water and frozen) and observed which part of the hand melts first. Can anything be added to the gloves/balloons to speed up melting?

- Explored which liquids cool the fastest.

- Measured the temperature of water in different state of matter.

- Observed evaporation in everyday situations.

- Observed condensation in everyday situations (sleet, hail, snow, water on a cold can of fizzy drink, car windscreen on a cold day and mirrors when having a bath or shower).

- Explored the rate of evaporation – puddles on playground, handprints on paper towels or a wall, liquids in different sized containers.

- Used secondary sources to explore the water cycle.

- Made models of the water cycle (good examples can be found on Pinterest).

- Explored how to speed up or slow down the speed at which ice melts – rescue a character from the ice, or keep the character in the ice – good idea to link to popular films, e.g. *Minions*.

'WOW WORDS'

Solid, liquid, gas, evaporation, condensation, particles, temperature, freezing, heating, cooling, Celsius, water cycle, melting, reversible change.

POSSIBLE NAIVE IDEAS THAT MAY NEED TO BE CHALLENGED

- Issues with the terms condensation and evaporation, melting and dissolving.

- Dissolving means the solid has disappeared.

- A balloon that has been inflated will be lighter.

- Clouds are made of gas.

- When water evaporates it dries up and vanishes.

A POSSIBLE RICH TASK TO EVIDENCE 'SECURE MASTERY' OF CONCEPTS

Provide the children with two beakers: one where the water is frozen and the other where the water is still a liquid (water is mixed with salt). Remember – they should both have just come out of the freezer and please be aware of the possible risks of ice burns. Ask the children to explain why they think they are different. How can you explore this? If children know that the water may have salt dissolved in it, does it work for other solutions, e.g. sugar and water etc.? Can salt water freeze?

APPLICATION – USE SKILLS FROM BLOOM'S TAXONOMY – SKILL BEYOND RECALL

Using the skill of evaluation and synthesis, will consider the differences in solutions and freezing points using everyday experiences (e.g. will know why we add salt or other minerals on the roads when icy conditions are predicted, as shown in Figure 9.3). Will be able to manipulate variables in order to investigate salt solutions.

LOOKING FOR EVIDENCE OF MASTERY AT GREATER DEPTH

- Will know that water freezes at zero, so something must be different about the properties of this water.

- Will use evidence from their investigation to explain that water solutions freeze at a lower temperature than pure water.

SOUND

ATTAINMENT TARGETS FROM THE NATIONAL CURRICULUM'S PROGRAMME OF STUDY

- identify how sounds are made, associating some of them with something vibrating
- recognise that vibrations from sounds travel through a medium to the ear
- find patterns between the pitch of a sound and features of the object that produced it
- find patterns between the volume of a sound and the strength of the vibrations that produced it
- recognise that sounds get fainter as the distance from the sound source increases.

(DfE, 2014, p187)

TYPICAL ACTIVITIES USUALLY ASSOCIATED WITH OR USED IN LESSONS

- Undertaken a sound walk around the school.

- Explored making sounds with a range of musical instruments and other objects.

- Explored string telephones.

- Changed the pith of the sounds – different sized drums or saucepans, changing the length and thickness on a stringed instrument (elastic band box), bottles of water with different amounts of water.

- Made their own pitched musical instrument.

- Measured sound over distances.

- Measured sounds through different types of material and made their own ear muffs or sound-proofed shoe box.

- Explained and tested how sound can be reduced.

'WOW WORDS'

Vibration, volume, pitch, medium, insulation.

POSSIBLE NAIVE IDEAS THAT MAY NEED TO BE CHALLENGED

- Sound cannot travel through solids.

- How sound travels.

- What is vibrating – may think it is the air, rather than the solid.

A POSSIBLE RICH TASK TO EVIDENCE 'SECURE MASTERY' OF CONCEPTS

Present the children with a picture of two different thickness of elastic bands – one thick and one thinner but both the same length. Around the outside have several speech bubbles, one saying the thinner band will make the lower pitch sound; one saying they will be different pitches but will have the same volume; one saying they can be made to be the same pitch but will have different volumes; and have at least one blank for the children's own ideas to be included. Ask them to discuss what they think; is anyone correct (see Figure 9.4)?

The thinner the band, the lower the pitch.	The pitch will be different but they will have the same volume.

The elastic bands can be made to have the same pitch but will have different volumes.	Other ideas

Figure 9.4

(Picture sourced from Pixabay: https://pixabay.com/)

APPLICATION – USE SKILLS FROM BLOOM'S TAXONOMY – SKILL BEYOND RECALL

This task requires the children to evaluate their learning from making musical instruments and apply it to the problem in the abstract. In order to answer the question they need to have a deep understanding of the factors that impact pitch and volume.

LOOKING FOR EVIDENCE OF MASTERY AT GREATER DEPTH

- Will know how to alter the pitch and the volume when plucking strings.

- Will be able to identify patterns in pitch (can make the bands make the same sound by shortening the length of the band).

- Will know that a thinner band will make a higher pitched sound when compared to a thick band of the same length, therefore will know that a smaller drum will make a higher-pitched sound than a larger drum or that a smaller recorder will make a higher-pitched sound than a larger recorder.

ELECTRICITY

ATTAINMENT TARGETS FROM THE NATIONAL CURRICULUM'S PROGRAMME OF STUDY

- identify common appliances that run on electricity
- construct a simple series electrical circuit, identifying and naming its basic parts, including cells, wires, bulbs, switches and buzzers
- identify whether or not a lamp will light in a simple series circuit, based on whether or not the lamp is part of a complete loop with a battery
- recognise that a switch opens and closes a circuit and associate this with whether or not a lamp lights in a simple series circuit
- recognise some common conductors and insulators, and associate metals with being good conductors.

(DfE, 2014, p188)

TYPICAL ACTIVITIES USUALLY ASSOCIATED WITH OR USED IN LESSONS

- Listed a number of common appliances around the school and home that use electricity.

- Explored how the appliances work – sorted appliances into those that are battery-powered and those that use mains power.

- Identified and named components in a circuit.

- Explored how a circuit works (drama links).

- Sorted and classified materials into conductors and insulators.

- Explored which materials can be used instead of wires in a circuit.

- Explored switches and know how they work.

- Used knowledge of insulators and conductors to make own switches so that a bulb can be switched on and off.

- Made circuits linked to design and technology projects – e.g. motorised vehicle, made burglar alarms or considered how e-textiles work.

'WOW WORDS'

Cells, wires, bulbs, switches, battery, buzzers, circuit, series, conductors, insulators, components, brighter, dimmer.

POSSIBLE NAIVE IDEAS THAT MAY NEED TO BE CHALLENGED

- Understanding of how electricity 'flows' in a circuit – that it comes out of both ends of a battery and collides.

- Adding more bulbs to a circuit makes them brighter.

- Adding more buzzers makes a louder sound.

A POSSIBLE RICH TASK TO EVIDENCE 'SECURE MASTERY' OF CONCEPTS

Present the children with the circuit diagram shown in Figure 9.5.

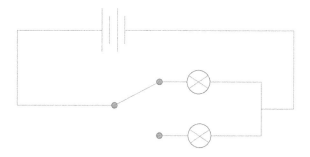

Figure 9.5

Have speech bubbles around the outside, one saying 'I don't think the light bulbs will light as the electricity will escape out of the open side'; one saying 'I think both bulbs will light'; one saying 'I don't think it is possible to light both bulbs at the same time'; and have at least one blank speech bubble for the children to record their thoughts. Ask the children to discuss what they think; who is correct?

APPLICATION – USE SKILLS FROM BLOOM'S TAXONOMY – SKILL BEYOND RECALL

This task requires pupils to evaluate their knowledge of switches and apply it to the diagram to work out which light bulb would light. Some will take it further and consider/create a circuit similar to the one where both light bulbs could be lit.

LOOKING FOR EVIDENCE OF MASTERY AT GREATER DEPTH

- Will know that a switch opens or closes a circuit and associate this with whether or not a bulb will light.

10

ACTIVITIES LINKED TO THE NATIONAL CURRICULUM: YEAR 5

LIVING THINGS AND THEIR HABITATS

ATTAINMENT TARGETS FROM THE NATIONAL CURRICULUM'S PROGRAMME OF STUDY

- describe the differences in the life cycles of a mammal, an amphibian, an insect and a bird
- describe the life process of reproduction in some plants and animals.

(DfE, 2014, p192)

Figure 10.1

(Picture sourced from Pixabay: https://pixabay.com/)

TYPICAL ACTIVITIES USUALLY ASSOCIATED WITH OR USED IN LESSONS

- Used secondary sources and observations to find out about life cycles.

- Identified patterns in life cycles in plants and animals from around the world.

- Drawn life cycles of a range of animals – identified similarities and differences.

- Compared gestation periods for animals and looked for patterns (e.g. size of animals and time for dependency).

- Compared the life cycles of two or more types of animals, e.g. amphibians with birds.

- Explained how a range of plants reproduce asexually.

- Planted bulbs – dividing plants such as daffodils.

- Taken cuttings from plants (e.g. mint) to grow (asexual reproduction).

- Explored concepts about pollination and fertilisation.

'WOW WORDS'

Mammal, insect, reproduction, juvenile, dependency, maturity, offspring, asexual reproduction, pollination, fertilisation.

POSSIBLE NAIVE IDEAS THAT MAY NEED TO BE CHALLENGED

- Understanding of the different stages of a life cycle and associated terminology.
- Understanding of the differences between sexual and asexual reproduction.

A POSSIBLE RICH TASK TO EVIDENCE 'SECURE MASTERY' OF CONCEPTS

Show the children a picture of a flowering potato plant (see Figure 10.1). Ask the children what would happen if we planted the seeds from the potato plant? Would we get a potato plant? Would it be exactly the same as the parent plant? What would happen if we planted a potato? Would we get a potato plant? How would it be different from the plant planted from a seed? Can this be done with any other plants?

APPLICATION – USE SKILLS FROM BLOOM'S TAXONOMY – SKILL BEYOND RECALL

This requires the children to have a deep understanding of reproduction. Children who have mastered this will be able to apply their learning and evaluate that the seed plant has more possibility for variation if it is cross-pollinated, whereas the tuber will be a direct copy.

LOOKING FOR EVIDENCE OF MASTERY AT GREATER DEPTH

- Will be able to explain the differences between sexual and asexual reproduction.

- Will know that plants can reproduce in both ways (tubers – asexual, flowers and seeds – sexual).

ANIMALS INCLUDING HUMANS

ATTAINMENT TARGETS FROM THE NATIONAL CURRICULUM'S PROGRAMME OF STUDY

- describe the changes as humans develop to old age.

(DfE, 2014, p192)

TYPICAL ACTIVITIES USUALLY ASSOCIATED WITH OR USED IN LESSONS

- Constructed timelines with approximate timings for each stage of the life cycle.

- Explained changes at various points during the life cycle, e.g. puberty and changes in boys and girls.

- Links to PSHCE and policy on Relationships and Sex Education.

'WOW WORDS'

Foetus, embryo, womb, gestation, baby, toddler, teenager, elderly, growth, development, puberty.

POSSIBLE NAIVE IDEAS THAT MAY NEED TO BE CHALLENGED

- Understanding of vocabulary linked to life cycle.

- Understanding that different plants and animals have differences in the time spent in various stages (e.g. humans have a prolonged childhood).

A POSSIBLE RICH TASK TO EVIDENCE 'SECURE MASTERY' OF CONCEPTS

Present the children with the human life cycle. Ask them to compare it with the life cycles of a cat and an elephant (see Figure 10.2). Get the children to evaluate the similarities and differences. Ask the children why they think there are similarities between these three animals (see Figure 10.3). See if the children make the link to them all being mammals; if so, ask them if this life-cycle pattern is the same for all mammals.

Figure 10.2

(Pictures sourced from Pixabay: https://pixabay.com/)

SIX STAGES OF THE HUMAN LIFE CYCLE

1. Gestation (foetus growing in womb, typically 40 weeks)

2. Baby (after birth)

3. Childhood (learning to walk and talk)

4. Adolescence (teenage years)

5. Adulthood (body is fully developed)

6. Old age (last stage of the human life cycle)

Figure 10.3

(Pictures sourced from Pixabay: https://pixabay.com/)

APPLICATION – USE SKILLS FROM BLOOM'S TAXONOMY – SKILL BEYOND RECALL

This requires the children to have a deep understanding of the stages of life in the human life cycle. They need to use the evaluation skills to compare ideas to other mammals and analyse why differences might exist, e.g. the time spent as a juvenile (this is extended in humans and children may consider why this is the case).

LOOKING FOR EVIDENCE OF MASTERY AT GREATER DEPTH

- Will be able to describe the changes that mammals go through over the duration of a life cycle and will consider similarities and differences.

- Will be able to ascribe approximate timings for each life cycle and will be able to explain why the life cycles of mammals differ.

- Will be able to identify patterns in life cycles.

PROPERTIES AND CHANGES

ATTAINMENT TARGETS FROM THE NATIONAL CURRICULUM'S PROGRAMME OF STUDY

- compare and group together everyday materials on the basis of their properties, including their hardness, solubility, transparency, conductivity (electrical and thermal), and response to magnets
- know that some materials will dissolve in liquid to form a solution, and describe how to recover a substance from a solution
- use knowledge of solids, liquids and gases to decide how mixtures might be separated, including through filtering, sieving and evaporating
- give reasons, based on evidence from comparative and fair tests, for the particular uses of everyday materials, including metals, wood and plastic
- demonstrate that dissolving, mixing and changes of state are reversible changes
- explain that some changes result in the formation of new materials, and that this kind of change is not usually reversible, including changes associated with burning and the action of acid on bicarbonate of soda.

(DfE, 2014, p193)

TYPICAL ACTIVITIES USUALLY ASSOCIATED WITH OR USED IN LESSONS

- Investigated properties to recommend for a particular function, e.g. thermal insulators – which materials are best to keep a cup of tea or jacket potato warm?

- Explored materials and shown in-depth awareness of why they have chosen the material, e.g. plastic ruler being better than a glass ruler (although both are transparent).

- Observed which solids dissolve in liquid.

- Measured rates if dissolving by changing variables.

- Separated materials by filtering, sieving and/or evaporating (could make global links here to clean drinking water).

- Investigated non-reversible changes, e.g. rusting, cooking (cakes, bread), acids when mixed with bicarbonate of soda, bath bombs.

- Sorted cards to show which reactions are reversible and which are non-reversible.

- Explored the work of scientists.

'WOW WORDS'

Hardness, solubility, solution, transparency, conductivity, filter, evaporation, sieve, melting, dissolving, mixing, burning, non-reversible, reversible, insulator, conductor.

POSSIBLE NAIVE IDEAS THAT MAY NEED TO BE CHALLENGED

- Language issues – filtering, sieving, conductors, insulators.

A POSSIBLE RICH TASK TO EVIDENCE 'SECURE MASTERY' OF CONCEPTS

Present the children with the following problem: At a local factory the forklift truck went out of control and tipped its load into the drinking water tank. The forklift truck was carrying salt, sugar,

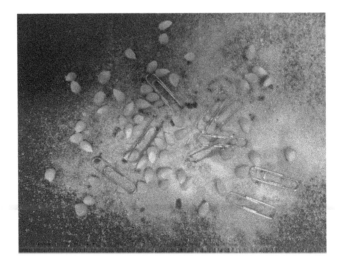

Figure 10.4

sand, paper clips, drawing pins and popping corn (see Figure 10.4). Ask the children if they could explain to the owner of the factory how they can clear the drinking water so as not to waste it. The owner has also asked if it is possible to get back each of these items separately from the water. Ask the children to justify their response to this question.

APPLICATION – USE SKILLS FROM BLOOM'S TAXONOMY – SKILL BEYOND RECALL

This requires the children to apply their knowledge of mixtures and solutions and how they can be separated. It also requires them to evaluate whether it is possible to separate materials with similar properties, e.g. salt and sugar as both dissolve in water.

LOOKING FOR EVIDENCE OF MASTERY AT GREATER DEPTH

- Will use knowledge of solids and liquids to decide how to separate a mixture, including through filtering, sieving and evaporating.

- Will know which materials dissolve in liquids (salt and sugar) and that filtration and sieving will not separate them in a mixture.

EARTH AND SPACE

ATTAINMENT TARGETS FROM THE NATIONAL CURRICULUM'S PROGRAMME OF STUDY

- describe the movement of the Earth, and other planets, relative to the Sun in the solar system
- describe the movement of the Moon relative to the Earth
- describe the Sun, Earth and Moon as approximately spherical bodies
- use the idea of the Earth's rotation to explain day and night and the apparent movement of the sun across the sky.

(DfE, 2014, p194)

TYPICAL ACTIVITIES USUALLY ASSOCIATED WITH OR USED IN LESSONS

- Created a model or role play to show the movement of the Earth around the Sun and the Moon around the Earth.

- Modelled day and night using secondary sources and made short videos to explain the animation.

- Used first-hand observations of shadow length over the day.

- Made a sundial to explore the apparent movement of the Sun across the sky.

- Researched time zones to explain when it is night and day in different countries.

- Produced diagrams to show how rotations of the Earth cause day and night.

- Researched scientists of the past.

- Researched planets in the solar system and produced a fact file or poem.

- Used secondary sources to reason why the Sun, Earth and Moon are spherical.

- Produced own Moon diaries.

'WOW WORDS'

Earth, Sun, Moon, axis, rotation, day, night, phases of the moon, star, sphere, planet, dwarf planet, Mercury, Venus, Mars, Jupiter, Saturn, Uranus and Neptune.

POSSIBLE NAIVE IDEAS THAT MAY NEED TO BE CHALLENGED

- The Moon changes shape due to the shadow of the Earth.

- The Sun comes up and goes down.

- The Earth goes around the Sun to give day and night.

- Pluto is a planet.

A POSSIBLE RICH TASK TO EVIDENCE 'SECURE MASTERY' OF CONCEPTS

Present the children with a picture of the Earth (part in the light and part in the dark; see Figure 10.5). Around the outside have a range of speech bubbles, one that says 'I think the Earth must spin clockwise in order to have night and day (when looking down from the North Pole)'; another saying 'I think the Earth must spin anticlockwise in order to have night and day (when looking down from the North Pole)'; another saying 'It does not matter which way it spins as there will still be night and day'; and a final one saying 'It does not spin. It is the Sun that moves, which gives us night and day'. You might also like to include some blank speech bubbles for the children's ideas. Ask them to discuss what they think.

APPLICATION – USE SKILLS FROM BLOOM'S TAXONOMY – SKILL BEYOND RECALL

This task requires the children to recall their knowledge about the Sun's apparent movement across the sky and apply it to this problem. They need to evaluate/recreate in which direction it must spin in order for the Sun to rise in the east and set in the west.

I think the Earth must spin clockwise in order to have night and day (when looking down from the North Pole).

I think the Earth must spin anticlockwise in order to have night and day (when looking down from the North Pole).

It does not matter which way it spins as there will still be night and day.

It does not spin. It is the Sun that moves, which gives us night and day.

Figure 10.5

(Picture sourced from Pixabay: https://pixabay.com/)

LOOKING FOR EVIDENCE OF MASTERY AT GREATER DEPTH

- Will know how the Earth spins on its axis over 24 hours to give us day and night.

- Will use their understanding of sunrise and sunset to consider the direction of spin of the Earth.

FORCES AND MAGNETS

ATTAINMENT TARGETS FROM THE NATIONAL CURRICULUM'S PROGRAMME OF STUDY

- explain that unsupported objects fall towards the Earth because of the force of gravity acting between the Earth and the falling object
- identify the effects of air resistance, water resistance and friction, that act between moving surfaces
- recognise that some mechanisms, including levers, pulleys and gears, allow a smaller force to have a greater effect.

(DfE, 2014, p195)

Figure 10.6

(Picture sourced from Pixabay: https://pixabay.com/)

TYPICAL ACTIVITIES USUALLY ASSOCIATED WITH OR USED IN LESSONS

- Observed how unsupported objects fall.

- Investigated friction in different contexts – trainers, bath mats, slides, different running surfaces (see Figure 10.6).

- Investigated the effect of water resistance by dropping shapes through water, pulling shapes along the surface of water.

- Investigated air resistance using parachutes, spinners, sails on land yachts and yachts.

- Explored how levers and pulleys work.

'WOW WORDS'

Air resistance, water resistance, friction, gravity, Newton, gears, pulleys.

POSSIBLE NAIVE IDEAS THAT MAY NEED TO BE CHALLENGED

- Heavy objects fall faster than lighter objects.

- Light objects float.

- Friction is bad.

- An object that is still has no forces acting upon it.

A POSSIBLE RICH TASK TO EVIDENCE 'SECURE MASTERY' OF CONCEPTS

Explain to the children that they have been asked for their help by the head teacher. A local school has challenged the school to a running competition but the problem is they have some of the fastest runners in the county. The head teacher was wondering if the children could use their knowledge of forces to help them come up with ideas of how to slow down these runners. Get the children to produce a poster explaining what they would do, explaining how the science will help to slow the runners down. Remind the children that there may be more than one method of slowing the runners down.

APPLICATION – USE SKILLS FROM BLOOM'S TAXONOMY – SKILL BEYOND RECALL

This activity requires the children to first evaluate the forces acting on a person who is running. They then need to apply their knowledge of these forces in order to synthesise ideas which will cause these to become greater and slow the runner down. For example: if they get the person to run with their jacket open this will cause more air resistance than if it was zipped up. They could also consider the impact of different running surfaces or trainer sole.

LOOKING FOR EVIDENCE OF MASTERY AT GREATER DEPTH

- Will know how to increase frictional forces to slow a runner down.

- Will know that air resistance is a frictional force and can slow movement.

11

ACTIVITIES LINKED TO THE NATIONAL CURRICULUM: YEAR 6

LIVING THINGS AND THEIR HABITATS

TYPICAL ACTIVITIES USUALLY ASSOCIATED WITH OR USED IN LESSONS

- Know about the classification system and why it is important. There are some nice links between descriptive writing in English and classification that could be made. Children could write descriptions of animals and will think about the issues of doing this from a scientific perspective. This task would be a good link to the formal classification system and the work of Carl Linnaeus.

Figure 11.1

(Picture sourced from Pixabay: https://pixabay.com/)

- Grouped living things according to groups – classification system.

- Observed characteristics shared by animals in a group.

- Assigned animals to groups.

- Used Venn diagrams to classify and sort animals and plants.

- Provided examples of flowering non-flowering plants.

- Created classification keys for plants and animals.

- Created imaginary animals and assigned them to taxonomic groups.

'WOW WORDS'

Classification, vertebrates, invertebrates, micro-organisms, amphibians, reptiles, mammals, insects.

POSSIBLE NAIVE IDEAS THAT MAY NEED TO BE CHALLENGED

- Confusion between terms such as vertebrates and invertebrates.

- Understanding the differences between living things and why they are grouped as they are.

A POSSIBLE RICH TASK TO EVIDENCE 'SECURE MASTERY' OF CONCEPTS

Provide the children with a tray that has sand in it and in different layers of the sand place pictures of fossil fragments (e.g. skeleton, plant, or inspect parts; see Figure 11.1). If you wish to use real bones please see the *ASE Be Safe* book for guidance. Use an animal they have not studied. Give the children small brushes and explain that they are going to be archaeologists and discuss what animals lived here in the past. Are the children able to use their previous knowledge to put things back together? Can they explain what it was? Which group does it belong to? How do they know? Why does it not belong to another group? How would it be similar and or different?

APPLICATION – USE SKILLS FROM BLOOM'S TAXONOMY – SKILL BEYOND RECALL

This activity requires the children to first have a secure knowledge of the different groups of living things. It requires them to use this knowledge to create the discovered item and evaluate this against the groups of living things they studied in order to decide what group it is most likely to belong to. Children may use classification materials to help them to identify unknown animals.

LOOKING FOR EVIDENCE OF MASTERY AT GREATER DEPTH

•   Will be able to use their understanding of the five taxonomic groups of vertebrate animals (bird, mammal, amphibian, reptile or fish) or invertebrates (insects, arachnid, crustacean, snail, worm etc.) to identify which group the fossil belongs to.

•   Will be able to explain and justify why the animal should be in a certain group using key scientific vocabulary associated with observable features and characteristics of the animal group.

ANIMALS INCLUDING HUMANS

Figure 11.2

(Picture sourced from Pixabay: https://pixabay.com/)

ATTAINMENT TARGETS FROM THE NATIONAL CURRICULUM'S PROGRAMME OF STUDY

- identify and name the main parts of the human circulatory system, and describe the functions of the heart, blood vessels and blood
- recognise the impact of diet, exercise, drugs and lifestyle on the way their bodies function
- describe the ways in which nutrients and water are transported within animals, including humans.

(DfE, 2014, p196)

TYPICAL ACTIVITIES USUALLY ASSOCIATED WITH OR USED IN LESSONS

- Drawn diagrams of the circulatory system and labelled key organs.
- Made a simple model of the heart (threading red or blue coloured wool through the chambers of the heart is a good way to show that the heart is a double pump).
- Know that the heart transports nutrients as well as gases and water.
- Role play to explain main parts of circulatory system (double pump).
- Conducted a fair test to explore the effect of pulse rate when engaging in different activities.
- Explored recovery rates after exercise.
- Produced a leaflet describing impact on drugs and lifestyle on the body (includes impact of caffeine).
- Engaged with a visitor from police/school nurse to discuss drugs and/or healthy lifestyles.

'WOW WORDS'

Circulatory system, heart, blood, arteries, veins, vessels, oxygenated, deoxygenated, valve, carbon dioxide, nutrients, muscles, exercise, respiration, nutrients, diet, drugs, harmful, beneficial.

POSSIBLE NAIVE IDEAS THAT MAY NEED TO BE CHALLENGED

- Blood is blue in the veins and red in the arteries.
- Positioning and size of organs in the circulatory system.
- The heart only beats faster when we exercise in order to work our muscles.

A POSSIBLE RICH TASK TO EVIDENCE 'SECURE MASTERY' OF CONCEPTS

Give the children a picture of a person sitting in a chair (resting). Around the outside have the following speech bubbles: 'Everyone's heart beats at the same rate when they are at rest'; 'If you do not exercise regularly your heart beats more slowly when you are resting'; 'If you exercise a lot then your heart will beat faster when you are resting'; and a blank speech bubble for the children's ideas.

APPLICATION – USE SKILLS FROM BLOOM'S TAXONOMY – SKILL BEYOND RECALL

This task requires the children to have a deep understanding of the effects of exercise on the human heart. They will need to evaluate what they know about the effects of exercise on the heart (e.g. heart beats faster during exercise to deliver oxygen, nutrients, and remove waste products), however, when at rest the heart can beat slower. People who exercise regularly often have lower resting heart rates, e.g. Usain Bolt is said to have a resting heart rate of 33 beats a minute.

LOOKING FOR EVIDENCE OF MASTERY AT GREATER DEPTH

- Will have an understanding of why the heart beasts faster during exercise.

- Will know that different activities impact upon how fast the heart beats.

- Will know that nutrients and oxygen are pumped around the body to the muscles (and other parts of the body).

- Will know that carbon dioxide is taken back to the heart to be removed from the body by the lungs.

EVOLUTION AND INHERITANCE

ATTAINMENT TARGETS FROM THE NATIONAL CURRICULUM'S PROGRAMME OF STUDY

- recognise that living things have changed over time and that fossils provide information about living things that inhabited the Earth millions of years ago
- recognise that living things produce offspring of the same kind, but normally offspring vary and are not identical to their parents
- identify how animals and plants are adapted to suit their environment in different ways and that adaptation may lead to evolution.

(DfE, 2014, p197)

TYPICAL ACTIVITIES USUALLY ASSOCIATED WITH OR USED IN LESSONS

- Matched animals to habitats and explained why they are suited to live there.

- Explained how animals are adapted to environments, e.g. desert rats having large ears, polar bear having thick coat etc. Used a graphic organiser to explain how parts of the animals help it to live in its habitat.

- Explored Darwin's finches and Galapagos tortoises and how they are adapted to the different islands.

- Researched how animals have evolved over time, e.g. giraffe through natural selection.

- Compared skeletons – looking at limbs of different animals – considered what is similar or different. Chosen an animal and made a model of the limbs using plasticine.

- Designed a new plant or animals adapted to live in an unusual habitat, e.g. bookcase, bones or fruit.

- Researched the peppered moth and know why the colour changed over a short period of time (camouflage and protection).

- Considered fossil evidence – matched fossils to pictures of the animals or plant when living. Worked as a palaeontologist to piece together bones to make an animal.

- Made their own fossils using the cast and mould technique.

- Compared the work of Darwin and Wallace.

- Looked at family pictures or those of celebrity families (where appropriate) and identified similar features.

- Will know what makes a rose a rose, and may look at different species of dogs – could link to the dog show Crufts.

'WOW WORDS'

Fossils, adaptation, evolution, characteristics, reproduction, genetics, environment, palaeontologist, advantage, disadvantage, species.

POSSIBLE NAIVE IDEAS THAT MAY NEED TO BE CHALLENGED

- A giraffe has a long neck because it stretches to reach the higher leaves.

- A polar bear has a thick coat because it lives in a cold climate.

- Girls look like their mum and boys look like their dad.

A POSSIBLE RICH TASK TO EVIDENCE 'SECURE MASTERY' OF CONCEPTS

Give the children some plasticine in different colours. Ask them to create an animal who lives in the flower bed and eats ants (see Figure 11.3). Explain that this animal has no predators. Discuss the creations with the children, asking them to explain why they have included different features. Explore if these are based on their understanding of existing animals, e.g. an anteater's long tongue to collect up the termites efficiently.

Explain to the children that a bird has been introduced into the habitat, which likes to eat this animal. Ask them to show how their animal might adapt so that the bird does not eat them. Children might make a short presentation explaining the adaptions.

Figure 11.3

APPLICATION – USE SKILLS FROM BLOOM'S TAXONOMY – SKILL BEYOND RECALL

This activity requires the children to have a deep understanding of 'survival of the fittest' in order to create an animal who could survive in a particular habitat. In addition, they recognise that animals adapt as their habitat changes. Those with a deeper understanding of evolution will realise that this takes several generations because those who survive with the desired traits go on to breed and pass these traits on to their offspring.

LOOKING FOR EVIDENCE OF MASTERY AT GREATER DEPTH

- Will be able to explain the process of how their Blobster is suited to an environment and how and why it may change and evolve over time.

- Will know that changes may be essential to survival over rivals (survival of the fittest) and results in evolution.

- Will know that the change will take several generations and that changes in a species occurs because desirable traits are passed on to subsequent generations (desirable traits are inherited).

LIGHT

Figure 11.4

(Picture sourced from Pixabay: https://pixabay.com/)

TYPICAL ACTIVITIES USUALLY ASSOCIATED WITH OR USED IN LESSONS

- Explored the different sources of light (recap from Year 3).

- Explored the way that light travels in straight lines by shining a torch down a hose pipe or using different shapes in card.

- Explored how light travels through different liquids.

- Made periscopes to understand how mirrors help you to see around corners (produced a labelled drawing to explain this).

- Explored what happens when objects are placed in water or other solids.

- Explored colours in soap bubbles (these change just before the bubble pops).

- Made shadow puppets using different materials and different distances form a light source.

- Used models and diagrams to explain the path of light rays.

- Explained, using drawing, how shadow-shape changes.

'WOW WORDS'

Refraction, reflection, light, spectrum, rainbow, colour, shadow.

POSSIBLE NAIVE IDEAS THAT MAY NEED TO BE CHALLENGED

- Eyes are active organs in the seeing process.

A POSSIBLE RICH TASK TO EVIDENCE 'SECURE MASTERY' OF CONCEPTS

This problem is based on an old SATs question which children found difficult. Present the children with a picture of a turtle on a moonlit beach (see Figure 11.4). Around the outside of the picture have some speech bubbles, e.g. one saying 'You can see the turtle because the Moon is a light source'; one saying 'Our eyes produce light at night to help us see the turtle'; one saying 'The turtle produces light which is why we can see it'; and also have a blank bubble. Ask the children why they think it is possible to see the turtle at night? Can they draw a diagram to support their ideas? Would it be possible to see the turtle if there was no moon in the sky?

APPLICATION – USE SKILLS FROM BLOOM'S TAXONOMY – SKILL BEYOND RECALL

In order to answer this problem, children need a deep understanding of how the eye functions. They also know that the Moon is not a light source but is just reflecting the Sun's light. The children will be able to evaluate this and show the light reflects off the Moon, which reflects off the turtle and into the eye. They will be able to clearly explain that without the reflected light of the Moon it may be impossible to see the turtle unless there is another source of light.

LOOKING FOR EVIDENCE OF MASTERY AT GREATER DEPTH

- Will be able to describe how we see the turtle.

- Will draw a diagram to show the path of the light rays.

- Will know that light is reflected off objects into our eyes.

- Will know that if there is no light source, we will not be able to see the turtle.

- Will know that the Moon is not a light source but reflected light.

ELECTRICITY

ATTAINMENT TARGETS FROM THE NATIONAL CURRICULUM'S PROGRAMME OF STUDY

- associate the brightness of a lamp or the volume of a buzzer with the number and voltage of cells used in the circuit
- compare and give reasons for variations in how components function, including the brightness of bulbs, the loudness of buzzers and the on/off position of switches
- use recognised symbols when representing a simple circuit in a diagram.

(DfE, 2014, p199)

Figure 11.5

(Picture sourced from Pixabay: https://pixabay.com/)

TYPICAL ACTIVITIES USUALLY ASSOCIATED WITH OR USED IN LESSONS

- Undertaken fair tests to explore changes in circuits.

- Made circuits as part of Design and Technology.

- Explored variations in circuits – changing brightness of bulb.

- Drawn circuit diagrams.

- Measured brightness of bulbs.

'WOW WORDS'

Cells, wires, bulbs, switches, buzzers, series, conductors, insulators, amps, volts, cell, symbols.

POSSIBLE NAIVE IDEAS THAT MAY NEED TO BE CHALLENGED

- Understanding of terms, e.g. voltage.

A POSSIBLE RICH TASK TO EVIDENCE 'SECURE MASTERY' OF CONCEPTS

Show the children a circuit which consists of two batteries and a light bulb. Explain that a Year 4 child wants to add three more bulbs to the circuit, but they are not as bright as when there is just one bulb. Is it possible to add more bulbs and still make them the same brightness? Ask the children to justify why their solution would work? Is there any other way of achieving the same outcomes? If the children physically explore the problem, be aware that cheap bulbs used in schools can often give unexpected or 'strange' results as the resistance is not consistent in each bulb.

APPLICATION – USE SKILLS FROM BLOOM'S TAXONOMY – SKILL BEYOND RECALL

There are several possible solutions to this problem so children who have a deep understanding of electricity will be able to identify both (e.g. bulbs in parallel or that have six batteries and bulbs in series). The children will have to use their knowledge of why and how components vary in a circuit to synthesise a solution to the problem

LOOKING FOR EVIDENCE OF MASTERY AT GREATER DEPTH

- Will be able to show how variations in how components work can be changed by increasing or decreasing the number of cells, different voltages etc.

- Will devise ways to measure the brightness of bulbs.

- Will work systematically to investigate a problem.

REFERENCES

Bird, S and Saunders, I (2007) *Rational Food*. Stafford: Millgate House Publications.

DfE (2014) *The National Curriculum in England: Framework Document*. London: DfE. Accessed at: https://assets.publishing.service.gov.uk/government/uploads/system/uploads/attachment_data/file/381344/Master_final_national_curriculum_28_Nov.pdf

INDEX

Page numbers in *italics* refer to figures; those in **bold** refer to tables.